A Sense of Permanence?

Essays on the Art of the Cartoon

A Sense of Permanence?

Essays on the Art of the Cartoon

Celebrating the 21st Anniversary of
The Centre for the Study of Cartoons and Caricature

The Centre for the Study of Cartoons and Caricature
University of Kent at Canterbury

First published in 1997 by
The Centre for the Study of Cartoons and Caricature,
University of Kent at Canterbury, Canterbury, Kent CT2 7NU
Distributed by Park McDonald.

Park McDonald is an imprint of Deirdre McDonald Books
7 Westhorpe Road, London SW15 1QH

Copyright © 1997 The Centre for the Study of Cartoons and Caricature
Essays copyright © the contributors
Cartoons copyright © see Acknowledgements

A CIP record for this book is available from the British Library

All rights reserved. No part of this publication may be reproduced
or transmitted in any form or by any means without permission.

ISBN 1 898094 20 9

Produced by The University of Kent at Canterbury Printing Unit.
Printed by Short Run Press Ltd, Exeter.

UNIVERSITY OF KENT
AT CANTERBURY ■■■■

Cover and frontispiece drawings: Ralph Steadman, *Between the Eyes* (Jonathan Cape, London, 1984) p.20, 13.
Back cover drawing: Victor Weisz ('Vicky'), 'The Cartoonist in Search of a Joke', *News Chronicle*, 20 February 1996.

A Sense of Permanence?

Essays on the Art of the Cartoon

Preface Robert Edwards	7
The Centre for the Study of Cartoons and Caricature and the University of Kent Colin Seymour-Ure	9
The End of The Line? The Future of British Cartooning John Jensen	11
It's No Laughing Matter to Some Ralph Steadman	23
One Thing After Another Steve Bell	31
An Interview with Nicholas Garland John Harvey	39
One Genuinely Universal Bit of Mischief Roger Law	45
Editorial Cartoons: A Transatlantic Perspective Kevin Kallaugher	53
Poison Pen or Good-Tempered Pencil? Humour and Hatred in 20th Century Political Cartoons Mark Bryant	59
Stiletto in the Ink: British Political Cartoons in the 1990s John Harvey	70
Contributors	79
Acknowledgements	80

Preface

Robert Edwards

Despite receiving an honorary doctorate from the University of Kent, and having spent the greater part of three decades excoriating his targets through cartoons, Ralph Steadman often wonders if it has all been worth the effort, or just a waste of everybody's time. 'In Britain', Steadman muses, 'they treat what you do as a rather menial task. Cartoons are somehow relegated to cheap third or fourth division stuff, far below writing.' To add insult to injury, he feels that many writers in this country consider cartoons disposable, 'a throwaway thing which cannot possibly have any other layers, undercurrents, or subtitles.' Since he considers his role that of a critical maverick 'playing outside the normal rules', Steadman hopes that one day cartoons will be granted a more lasting permanence – as 'something that wouldn't end up as fishwrap.'[1]

For over twenty years, The Centre for the Study of Cartoons and Caricature has endeavoured to preserve and promote the artistic heritage of Steadman and other mavericks like him. The Centre is the only archival resource of its kind in Britain which is dedicated to the championing of the cartoon as an historical artefact. To mark the 21st anniversary of its inauguration, the Centre has invited six of Britain's foremost cartoonists – along with a writer and a journalist – each to contribute an article which expresses their personal thoughts, feelings, premonitions, and forecasts on the cartoon profession.

The result is a collective anthology that aims to provide an insight into the political cartoon in Britain, as portrayed by the practitioners themselves. It also serves as a companion piece to the *20th Century Studies* issue published by the University in December 1975. Two of the original contributors to that issue, Professor Colin Seymour-Ure and the cartoonist John Jensen, are included here; the former providing an introductory overview of the Centre's history, the latter a personal and dark prediction of the cartoonist's future.

Steadman proceeds with his quasi-manifesto 'It's No Laughing Matter to Some', while Steve Bell inveighs against yellow journalism in 'One Thing After Another'. Nicholas Garland then describes his work's *raison d'être*, Roger Law of *Spitting Image* portrays his latex puppetry's universal popularity, and Kevin Kallaugher compares his cartooning experiences from a unique transatlantic perspective. These artists are then followed by Mark Bryant and John Harvey, who present an historian's review of 'hate' cartoons and a journalist's Reuter-Oxford research paper on British cartooning respectively. Whereas Jensen, Steadman, and Bell set a tone of alienated, often resigned pessimism, Harvey's 'Stiletto in Ink' concludes our anthology on an optimistic note, declaring that the art form has never been healthier. It will be left to the reader, in balancing these two perspectives, to reach his or her own conclusions.[2]

We are particularly grateful for the generous support extended to the Centre by the University of Kent Development Trust, which enabled the publication of this anthology to be realised. We also thank the University's Printing Unit, whose technical and graphic expertise was responsible for the production of this work.

Above all, we salute the contributors to this anthology. Their words and images are a testimony to a creative popular art form – an art form that, nevertheless, is to some in imminent danger of being undermined, if not extinguished altogether. We hope that this publication serves in its own way to provide the sense of permanence Steadman is looking for.

1. Ralph Steadman, interviewed in *The Times* (London, 22 August 1995), p. 10; *Telegraph Magazine* (London, 24 September 1994); *International Herald Tribune Weekend* (London, 6 January 1984), p. 7.
2. The fact that there are at present few, if any, female political cartoonists published on a regular basis in the major UK newspapers poses a question well worth exploring.

Why Not This Way?

'Perhaps the most exacting task of the portrait painter is that of keeping the sitter amused.' *Sir John Longstaff*

Will Dyson, Melboune *Punch*, ca. 1925.

The Centre for the Study of Cartoons and Caricature and the University of Kent

Colin Seymour-Ure

The Cartoon Centre began more like flu than a broken leg. With a leg, one minute it is not broken and the next minute it is. Flu, in contrast, creeps up on you. Thus did the idea for the Centre gradually take shape in the mind of its founder, Dr Graham Thomas, a member of Kent's Politics Department. His interest in inter-war anti-Fascist publications, such as Penguin Specials, was a background factor – and the Specials included three Low anthologies. Small incidents made a difference. Brian MacArthur, editor of the new *Times Higher Education Supplement*, sent a Kent colleague a Horner cartoon original about Kent's first student sit-in. This led Thomas to approach several cartoonists, including Ernest Shepard (by then in his nineties) and Leslie Illingworth, who lived not far away. Through Illingworth he met John Jensen, political cartoonist at the *Sunday Telegraph*, and Keith Mackenzie, Art Editor of Associated Newspapers. He became increasingly aware how ephemeral can be the life not only of a published cartoon but of the original artwork. Mackenzie and Jensen had recently collaborated for the British Cartoonists' Association on the magnificent exhibition, *Drawn and Quartered*, at the National Portrait Gallery. They too were struck by the precarious state of many collections, the disappearance of others, and the surprising lack of information about quite prominent cartoonists.

Mackenzie's interest led to the deposit at Kent in 1973 of 20,000 originals drawn for the *Daily Mail* and *Evening News*. Everyone likes cartoons, just as everyone thinks they have a sense of humour. So enthusiasm for Graham Thomas' proposal for a Cartoon Centre in the University quickly led to it being formalised. A grant from the Nuffield Foundation enabled two people to start work on cataloguing the collection for use.

The initial deposits included a marvellous range: classic sporting cartoons by Tom Webster, political cartoons by Bert Thomas, Joe Lee's 'London Laughs', Flook strips by Wally Fawkes (Trog). Lord Beaverbrook gets plaudits for his patronage of cartoonists, but the Harmsworths of Associated Newspapers deserve credit too. Individual cartoonists deposited their own originals, including large collections from Jensen and Nick Garland. Ernest Shepard gave one hundred of his drawings for *Punch* (and reminisced into the microphone). Emmwood gave several thousand drawings on retirement from the *Daily Mail*. The British Cartoonists' Association deposited drawings by the great *Daily Herald* artist, Will Dyson. Charles Roger, Cartoon Editor of the *Daily Mirror*, organised deposits by more than a dozen artists, including a long run of Andy Capps. When the *Express* papers were sold, a large collection of drawings by Strube, Low, Cummings and Vicky arrived, on the initiative of Beaverbrook's favourite historian, A.J.P. Taylor.

The defining moment when the University decided, so to speak, that it had caught a bug came with a formal inauguration one October evening in 1975. Lectures by Sir Ernst Gombrich and A.J.P. Taylor followed the opening of the exhibition *Getting Them In Line* by Jo Grimond, the University's Chancellor. The evening ended with half-a-dozen cartoonists (including Mark Boxer, who sadly is not represented in the archive) talking about their work to a room packed with cartoonists, journalists, staff, and students.

The cartoon as an area of study lies in 'a peculiar no-man's-land where several disciplines meet, and so [it] tends to be scorned by purists'.[1] This has probably made fundraising for the Cartoon Centre more difficult across the years, but the corresponding advantage has been flexibility in response to opportunities and to the needs of users. The remarkable computer catalogue, for example (now available on CD-ROM), for which the software has attracted awards and worldwide interest, is the product of initial curiosity by Computing Lecturer John Bovey and his wife Liz Ottaway. British historians of France, fishing for ways to mark the centennial of President De Gaulle's birth, were delighted when Kent's Julian Hurstfield was able to propose a cartoon exhibition. The result, sponsored by *The European*, was shown in London and France. When the Centre decided to research books on Low and Vicky, the Leverhulme Trust provided funds, and the National Portrait Gallery collaborated in two exhibitions which attracted record numbers of visitors.

All the Centre's work has come under one or other heading of research, teaching and curatorship. Top priority is to make the archive accessible. Scholars from all over the world come in search of visual material on anything from dentistry to musical instruments and national symbols (Russian bears, British lions). Others, including our own graduate students, study particular artists. Publishers, journalists, TV producers, hobbyists – even GCSE examiners – use the catalogue and library voraciously. The Centre's exhibitions travel nationally and abroad, and drawings are constantly in demand for loan. As funds allow, a priority programme for conservation of the most delicate artwork proceeds. The University's teaching draws on the Centre, and cartoonists come frequently to talk. Staff are in regular demand for lectures elsewhere.

The collection has nearly doubled since that defining day in 1975. Some material on loan will return to its owners after filming and cataloguing, to make way for additions. The search for financial support never stops. The Centre is an unrivalled national resource, unique in Britain and, probably, the world. Its work is also fun – and that as much as anything, one hopes, may gratify its generous supporters and ultimate *raison d'être*, the cartoonists themselves.

Reference

1. W.A.Coupe, 'Observations on a Theory of Political Caricature', *Comparative Studies in Society and History*, vol.II, 1969, p. 79.

The End of The Line?
The Future of British Cartooning

John Jensen

One makes one's little judgements – but nine times out of ten one is wrong.
Agatha Christie (Hercule Poirot), *Lord Edgware Dies*

Most professions suffer from too much jargon. Cartooning suffers from too little. The noun 'cartoon' covers humour as diverse as the Fat Slags in *Viz* to the most sophisticated creations of Steinberg in the *New Yorker*. It covers political, social, topical, gag and strip cartoons. To complicate matters each genre of cartooning has its own past and its own future. Under such circumstances generalisations can be misleading, but I will start with one: British cartooning has reached the end of an era. I am speaking particularly of the era of the gag or joke cartoon.

Cartoons are still drawn, published and laughed at in Britain; they thrive in Europe, Asia, America, Canada and Australia, yet with the closure of *Punch* in April 1992 an era came to an end and there doesn't seem to be a new one around to take its place. Cartoonists – wily, eelish creatures that they are – adapt to market changes and technological advances when they occur. When markets expand there are no problems, but when they contract adaptation becomes a matter of cunning and ingenuity, topped, of course, by talent.

John Lennon once remarked: 'Everything is happening but nothing's going on.' That sums up the state of cartooning in Britain today. New humour magazines have appeared and vanished; *Punch* has since revived, but whether its circulation will revive with it remains to be seen. There are now the Cartoon Art Trust Awards, and a Young Cartoonist of the Year Award. The Centre for the Study of Cartoons and Caricature at the University of Kent at Canterbury nurses plans for its future direction and growth. A course in Cartooning exists at the University of Central England, and cartoon workshops rise and fall all around. The Cartoon Art Trust exhibits home-grown cartoons as well as many from overseas. The social and professional interests of cartoonists are looked after by the Cartoonists' Club of Great Britain; The British Cartoonists' Association; The Cartoonists' Guild; FANNY (for female cartoonists world-wide); the Federation of European Cartoonists' Organisations (FECO) and the Association of Illustrators (AoI), which includes some cartoonists and humorous illustrators among its members.[1] Yet, British cartooning is in the doldrums. Over the next few years many gifted, young aspiring cartoonists will begin jostling the established professionals in the hope of placing enough work to make a decent living and a decent name for themselves.

After *Punch* briefly expired, two publications tried to replace it: *Squib* and *The Cartoonist*. Both failed. Only the *Oldie*, *Private Eye*, and the *Spectator*, and (approximately) two hundred and fifty other newspapers, magazines and specialist periodicals offer anything remotely like a cartoonist's haven.[2] This is a small haven considering that there are around one thousand working cartoonists[3] searching for markets. The number of magazines I have just given is misleading; not all of them are generous buyers. Some publish only a few regular cartoonists to the exclusion of all others. Others use syndicated cartoons as occasional space-fillers. A few pay as little as £25 per cartoon (I was often paid £20 per cartoon in the late fifties – the differential is enormous). Newspapers continue to publish political, social and topical cartoons, but the gag or joke cartoon – once the most common cartoon form of all – is now an endangered species.

Back to Before the Beginning

In 1944, Gombrich and Kris – wise observers of caricature – noted that 'though nearly every society known to us was acquainted with the comic on stage, in grotesque dances or in funny stories, far fewer of them knew comic pictures'.4 Drawn humour, when it finally arrived in our society, was quite different from other forms of visual humour. Why so long arriving? What was the difference? What was its strength? And does the difference and the strength hold any meaning in today's market place? Gombrich and Kris again: 'We think that portrait caricature was not practised earlier [than, say, the 16th century] because of the dire power it was felt to possess; out of the unconscious fear of its effect.'5 Today, poignant confirmation of that view comes from what was once Yugoslavia where the cartoonist Corax (Pedrag Koraksic), cartoonist of *Vreme*, is under threat of criminal proceedings following the publication of an unflattering caricature of the Serbian president Slobodan Milosevic. 'Forty years of experience in cartooning and caricaturing,' the artist is quoted as saying, 'have taught me that the more primitive a person is, the more he sees a caricature as an insult, and vice versa: the more he laughs at his own caricature, the less it bothers him.'6 In Britain the fear has gone, thank God, although people still say 'Magic!' when a drawing is quick-sketched before their eyes. One of *Punch*'s later Art Editors, Ken Taylor, used the word with feeling whenever a cartoon he particularly liked was put in front of him. But if the fear has gone the magic is also diminished; the magic has even changed hands. Nowadays, open-mouthed cartoonists – the computer illiterate ones – will stand in front of a monitor and cry 'Magic!' whilst people who 'cannot draw a line' produce stunning visuals with the aid of a mouse. The magic has been transferred from man to machine, or from caricaturist to virtually anyone who can handle a computer.

Whether on stage or on paper, day-to-day humour is mostly topical and therefore ephemeral. A mediaeval Rory Bremner could do his thing, yet once the act was over the humour was lost for ever along with the laughter and applause. Cartoons, good and bad, can last for centuries even when much of the original humour has dried out of them, the point has been lost or twisted in the passage of time. They can still be effective as drawings and as historical documents, but topical or not, dried out or not, the humour of cartoons is different from all other forms. A comedian's one-liner rarely can be translated into a successful drawing, whilst anyone trying to describe a cartoon verbally can be sure the humour will vanish in the telling.

At its most satisfying, pictorial humour is a reflective, ruminative art. Good cartoons are to be savoured. In Gillray's day rich men would buy or hire portfolios of satirical prints in order to study them at home, leisurely among friends: the drawings were talking points in an age of conversation. Today, paper is no longer the major recording material, and many homes are now more likely to keep and relish videos of 'Monty Python', 'Fawlty Towers', 'Absolutely Fabulous!', Rory Bremner or Dave Allen rather than today's cheaply produced, fast-ageing, quick-yellowing, easy disintegrating cartoon anthologies. Those varieties of spoken and acted humour which were once ephemeral are now (reasonably) permanent, cheap and available to all. Visual humour, like pictorial humour, can now be bought or hired, reflected upon, and savoured at leisure. The cartoonist's lone bid for immortality is now a shared experience diluted among many. The paper trail which began in the 15th century ends symbolically in front of the monitor. But before we come up to date let us take a look at another strength of the cartoonist to see how – or if – it is holding up over the years.

Down the centuries, whether his humour is coarse or refined, sweet or sour, the cartoonist's work has remained basically unchanged. Inevitably, today's targets are the same as yesterday's: politics, fashion, high and low society and personalities. Only the quality of the humour has altered.

The engravings of Gillray and his contemporaries were, as Dorothy M. George has remarked, 'virtually the only pictorial rendering of the flow of events...'[7] In Gillray's day satire flourished. Wit abounded. Squibs – the equivalent of *Private Eye* – were peddled cheaply and eagerly sought. It is worth noting that the theatre often played the part of today's tabloids. Ridicule and castigation were accepted in the theatre and were defended as 'the correction of individuals, and an example... to the whole community'[8] – a familiar justification for today's tabloid scurrility. In a smaller society personalities – whether royal, aristocratic or simply famously villainous – mixed more freely with the great mass of the people. Men and women of fashion were subjected to the same scrutiny as today's trendies, high-flyers, jet-setters, beautiful people and *Hello!* interviewees. The 'cits' – City merchants and tradesmen who made up an ever-increasing middle-class prototype of our yuppies, suits and fat-cats of today became well-known to the public through their appearances in the print-shop windows. Cartoonists still perform the same functions, but their role has been largely usurped by the media. Caricaturists' offerings have been largely replaced – rivalled – by pictures and stories in newspapers and their supplements, in magazines, photographs, films, television documentaries, sitcoms and even soaps. Visually, the rendering of the flow of events is an offering shared among many; subsequently, the once unique strength of the cartoonist is considerably weakened.

Are there other areas in which the cartoonist has lost out? We remind ourselves that pictorial humour was once 'the only pictorial rendering of the flow of events'. The artist/engraver, though far from rich, further from an assured income, and working in an 'inferior' art form, was nevertheless a centre of attention and controversy. Apart from providing comment, humour and satire, he was also a source of information and learning.

As every schoolboy knows, under the impetus of the Industrial Revolution society underwent a prolonged and radical transformation. The railways carried not only travellers throughout the land but also the novelty of illustrated national newspapers and magazines. As a consequence Britain, and indeed the rest of the world, became a smaller place. Line and halftone process reproduction, introduced towards the end of the nineteenth century, not only allowed drawings but also photographs of places and people to be distributed throughout the British Isles. Every new technological innovation from the 1840s to the 1990s has given cartoonists new areas of life, society and progress to comment upon: trains, cameras, the wireless, films, television – particularly television! – the Pill, computers, safe sex and Political Correctness. Such topics were, are, and will be meat for the newspaper cartoonist. Until recently they were often meat for the gag cartoonist too, but no longer. At least not in the same easy-going fashion, and for far fewer markets. Progress has always inspired countless jokes. However, these novelties (as each seemed at the time) were quietly, subtly and over a prolonged period undermining the gag cartoonists' power base.

Before the railways travel was difficult, dangerous and slow. There was no telling what might be found at the end of a journey, assuming you were not robbed or killed along the way. As the railways expanded, unknown landscapes revealed themselves. Other countries and cultures, no longer just dots on a map, became visible realities. Later, the wireless brought news, entertainment and knowledge into the home and at the same time was good for a thousand jokes. The cinema and the newsreels performed similar functions outside the home. Increasingly, the flow of history was recorded not only by cartoonists and caricaturists but by a fast proliferating media. One of the new amusements, a seemingly endless source of gags, was soon recognised as a social, domestic and political necessity: television. Television, however, was also the killer of the gag cartoon – the slow poison of the hapless gag merchant.

TV began, as far as most people are concerned, at the time of the Coronation of Queen Elizabeth II, when thousands of radio owners decided to buy or rent the then exciting new technology. It provided even greater amounts of variety and information, amusement, and news than any other medium. Readers became viewers, and as a result newspapers and magazines began to lose circulation. When commercial television appeared, advertisers raced to exchange the world of print for that of the cathode-ray tube. Circulations dropped even further and faster, as did advertising revenues. Down went *Picture Post*, *Lilliput*, *London Opinion*, *Men Only* (then a saucy but not salacious pocket-sized version), *John Bull*, *Illustrated*, *Everybody's*, the *Daily Sketch*, the (glossy) *Sketch*, the *Sunday Dispatch*, the *Weekend Mail* and so many more, confining with them to oblivion a huge gag-cartoon market. If desert islands, fakirs, monks, husbands-home-from-work, and rolling-pin-touting wives did not entirely disappear, they were no longer a major cartoon presence.

Unleashed in the late 50s, the contraceptive pill also began a process which played havoc with a host of income-providing stereotypes. The girlie-gag came under attack. With little fear of pregnancy, daughters were no longer tethered to mother's apron-strings and Dad found it increasingly difficult to insist that his brood, whether boys or girls, should be home by 10.30pm. Sexual liberation encouraged young people to break away from parental control and the many still-persisting Victorian attitudes. Echoes of Victorian life were not the noises young people wanted to hear, and the humour of *Punch*, if it was seen by them at all (which was unlikely), fell on eyes blinded by strobes. The girlie-gag, a staple of so many cartoons, rose from the coy he/she gags of the 1920s and earlier to the now boring secretary-on-Boss's knee jokes of the 1930s, 1940s and 1950s. Thence, arising from sexual liberation and a slackening of censorship, it proceeded to a latter-day Gillrayian coarseness and beyond; at which point Political Correctness head-butted the girls to the newsagents' top shelves. Again, television has shown us whatever areas of sex we may have missed while we were busy undergrounding our way through the sixties and seventies. So girlie gags still exist, but gone are the relatively innocent sauciness and wide, welcoming markets of *Blighty*, *Razzle*, *London Opinion* and the war-time *Men Only*. While these changes were taking place, *Punch* remained the great repository of the English Sense of Humour. But what was, or is, the English Sense of Humour?

The English Sense of Humour

The change from the bawdy world of Gillray and Rowlandson to discreet Victorianism was neatly symbolised by George Cruikshank, whose early, sharp-edged engravings underwent dramatic change when, ten years into Victoria's reign he – a heavy drinker – became teetotal. Whereupon, not only George Cruikshank sobered up but so did his work. He became genteel and polite. He became a Victorian. Cruikshank was not the last of the print engravers but with him, symbolically at least, the Golden Age of Caricature came to its end.

In parenthesis it should be noted that the priggishness of Victorian times never entirely eliminated the earlier coarseness, which not so much vanished as changed gear.

Some of its energy escaped into the vulgarity of the music halls, and something of the rollicking grotesqueries emerged in attenuated form in *Ally Sloper's Half-Holiday*, a weekly Victorian working-class comic of great vigour. Some – but by no means all! – of the bawdiness resurfaced in Donald McGill's postcards and, after injections of various substances from the sixties, it re-emerged again in the shape of *Private Eye* and *Oz*, and later *Viz* and *Zit* and similar earthy productions.

Victorian humour seemed to flow on a strong current. At the height of the Empire, national self-esteem and confidence rode high. Great Britain ruled the waves and much else. There was wealth, power and certainty. Yet English humour was modest and understated. It is easy to be modest and understated when you are sitting right on top of the heap and everyone knows their place and your voice is raised only at foreigners who fail to understand English.

Confidence and self-satisfaction bred a confident, self-satisfied sense of humour which, according to Harold Nicolson in his essay 'The English Sense of Humour', consisted of the following qualities and defects: good humour, tolerance, compassion; a fund of common sense; a gift for fancy; a respect for individual character rather than individual intelligence; a dislike of extremes; a love of games and play, which often assumes childish forms; self-consciousness and diffidence; a dislike of appearing conspicuous; laziness, especially intellectual laziness and optimism reflecting itself in a desire for mental and emotional ease. Here, surely, is a portrait of a nation at ease with itself – a nation bearing little resemblance to the Britain of today. The English Sense of Humour, born among the certitudes of Victorian Britain, survived and seemed to flourish for a while on post-war optimism and escapism – the desire to escape from the tedium of austerity. It survived, somehow, until the 60s smashed it in the teeth. *Punch*, reeling under the blow, teetered on as we know for three more decades.

What sort of market will a revived *Punch* seek? What pulse will its finger be on? Britain is no longer a comfortable, secure nation assured of its role in the world. Even now we still can't make up our mind whether to *really* go into Europe or to come out of it. At home, too many people have mortgages they cannot afford; or are saddled with negative equity or job insecurity. Part-time work and short-term contracts have kicked the traditional ladder of promotion from under swathes of high-flyers and security-seekers. The loneliness of working from home causes stress. Road rage, office rage, and domestic rage are everywhere. People raging at everything around them will be in no mood for quiet, reflective chuckles which insist that everything is for the best in the best of all possible worlds. Stressed-out victims of racism (even racists themselves!) and stressed-out parents (single or otherwise) trying to raise stressed-out children while their home benefit is being cut and unable to find a cure for their problems, may all seek whatever escapism they can find, but childlike whimsicality in a book of cartoons will not be a top priority. What will Mr Punch offer Brixton? Or Bradford? And Youth? 'Yoof' can climb on its bike and at the end of a week, a month or a lifetime find itself nowhere, except perhaps in a doorway. So 'Yoof' freaks out. People high on drugs or low after them are not in the market for cosy *Punch* like panaceas. Freakouts are as far removed from cosiness as a bush-fire from a suburban hearth. So where is our confidence now? Our pride in goals attained? Our anticipation of goals yet to be achieved? The kindliness and diffidence? Our sense of humour? If we seem to have lost our way, will the new technology help provide a new sense of purpose and direction?

Technological Progress within the Profession

Changes in British cartoon styles and adaptations of technique have arisen not so much through movements in fine art – unlike on the continent, these play a surprisingly small part in our cartoon history – but through technical changes in printing and production. The cartoonist evolved from the making of time-devouring, discipline-imposing metal engravings, in which a line carved in error might mean the destruction of the work of hours, perhaps days, to light etching and wood-engraving, to line-and-tone process engraving. The latter was the main means of reproduction stretching from the 1880s until the new technology of the 1980s.

At the British Cartoonists' Association dinner to honour the memory of the late Carl Giles, Peter Maddocks remarked that Giles worked in the best possible way at the best possible time.[9] He was usually three days behind the news and this worked to his and to his readers' advantage. Giles found a news story to his liking, drew his cartoon, sent it by rail to the *Daily Express,* and by the time it appeared in print the story had been seen and assimilated by the paper's readers. They therefore laughed not at the shock of the new but at recognition of the familiar.

Giles' work was reflective whilst most topical cartoonists are nowadays reflexive. Draughtsmanship has been stripped away. Observation and familiarity are merely sign-posted rather than pin-pointed. The function of the single-column topical cartoon – the pocket cartoon – is little more than a smiling exclamation point at the end of a news paragraph. It is a true function, with often funny results, but while they encourage wit they do little to encourage the Searles of this world, or the Steinbergs or Steadmans. Comic draughtsmen are also an endangered species.

The fax made possible the production of roughs, which can be seen and approved by editors within seconds. Finished drawings are also nowadays faxed to newspaper offices where they can be scanned and published immediately. An editor can commission a finished cartoon which will be drawn and accepted in little more time than it takes to make the drawing itself, which for some cartoonists these days is often no time at all. Speed, however, produces problems of its own. The cartoon and the news story on which it is based very often appear in the same paper on the same day. The reader usually goes to the picture first, which means that at times the cartoon is near meaningless until the story has been read and digested, by which time the particular impact of a tiny joke will have lost its savour. Technology has made the cartoonist too quick-witted by half, and the sharpest cartoonists are in danger of blunting their own wit.

Future Prospects

Writing in the *Writers' & Artists' Yearbook of 1996*, a determinedly upbeat John Byrne views the future optimistically – writing of 'lucrative merchandising... many opportunities'. According to Byrne, 'many cartoonists are certainly accomplished artists, but today funny ideas and sharp captions are just as important as the visuals. Writers with comic flair may consider collaborating with an artist or even trying their own simple drawings.' The phrase 'their own simple drawings' – their pictograms, perhaps – also seems to put cartoonists and their draughtsmanship quite low down the pecking order of achievement: an adjunct to thought rather than a spur.

Specialist and Trade publications are mentioned by Byrne as an under-exploited market. This may be true but not for long. In the University of Central England aspiring cartoonists are encouraged to think of working on corporate brochures, catalogues, guides, etc. These are all possible outlets, all possibly financially rewarding and which may breed successful careers. But is it challenging enough to bring bright new talents into the business when so much more fun can be had, and probably more money made, playing with computer images? When the several hundred entries to the 1996 Young Cartoonist of the Year were being judged, the judges noticed that the bulk of the entries were caricatures, comic-strip material or illustrations. Only a tiny minority of entrants sent in gag cartoons. The endangered species is not being nurtured by the young, so to whom or what can the gag cartoonist turn? To the Net?

The Internet

Already the Cartoonists' Guild is on the Internet. So too, among others, is the *Financial Times*. A recent letter from the *FT*, circulated to many of its illustrators, sums up the problem neatly. The *FT*'s syndication picture service has established a link with an electronic bulletin board with subscribers around the world. The *FT* says: 'In addition to sending pictures we also send graphics and it occurs to us that this could also be a way of marketing cartoons and line illustrations. At this stage we do not know just what returns we may get, but we feel that it is worth a try.' It is worth trying, and heartening, but it is also like hanging your paintings on the railings along London's Bayswater Road. A lot of paintings may have to be made for every sale. Hard work if you can get it.

The Internet, like syndication, can use only political and social cartoons which work on an international level. There is little room for parochial stuff in worldwide syndication. Gag cartoons, when sold internationally, have to satisfy the tastes of many countries where peoples' sensibilities, which vary from country to country, must not be upset. At source, most cartoonists are subject to 'voluntary' PC control. Therefore, pap must be produced. Excitement is discouraged, as is experiment. For many cartoonists there is no objection to this. Far from it. A seamless stream of gags for a reasonable return is a pleasant way to pass a life. The catch is that most syndicates, like most literary agents, whilst in theory welcoming new talent find it difficult in practice to make room for new talents – unless they are attached to a huge success like Gary Larson's 'The Far Side'. Most have more cartoon talent on their books than they can handle. The Internet is unlikely to be very different.

Going on the Internet brings cartoonists into the global market. Beyond the Globe there is nowhere to go: there are no Galactic bulletin boards. The view from Britain seems to be clear. Out there, somewhere, the possibility of 'new' markets can be tantalisingly glimpsed on-line in America, Canada, South America, Australia and New Zealand; in France, Germany, Italy and Spain; in the old Eastern Bloc countries; in Scandinavia. The trouble is that these countries feel the same way about us. They see us as a market, and they too are going on the Internet – if they are not already there.

The apparent newness of those markets is a mirage, not an oasis. When television was a novelty it was felt it would provide unlimited opportunities for cartoonists. It did not. Now we hope for unlimited opportunities from the Internet. But unless a new, unexpected, and unpredictable form of market appears, there are no new markets out there, just extant markets entrenched in countries filled with more than enough of their own cartoonists, caricaturists and illustrators.

Given some surface changes, the world market is fairly static – if one newspaper dies, another will take its place; if one publishing imprint is swallowed by a publishing giant, a minnow will begin publishing elsewhere. The number of cartoonists practising worldwide is probably fairly static, too. We are faced with a worldwide buyer's market. It is not the cartoonist who is facing new markets, but it is the buyer who is seeing hundreds, if not thousands, of 'new' cartoon talents worldwide. In the international buyer's market, the cartoonist – in whatever country he lives and works – is a number waiting to be called in a much bigger lottery than he has ever known.

Imagine the view from New Zealand. Out there is another young, ambitious David Low hoping – for example – that Britain will offer him further markets for his work. What markets? Our own barely exist. What happens if the editor of one of our nationals commissions work from this talented, distant being? Perhaps a work already finished, on-line, and awaiting its purchaser. What happens to that paper's regular, home-grown, freelance contributor? Will the sharp-eyed grey-suited men allow the editor to use both artists? Will he *want* to use both? Maybe he will prefer the New Zealander. And if the New Zealander is not the only newcomer but one among hundreds from that long list of countries, what then? The Internet could, conceivably, hammer our own markets even further into the ground.

Finally, there is the attitude of young people towards cartoons and cartooning. They do not object to cartoons, they probably find them funny when they do see them, but they do not go out of their way to look for them. They are not that interested. I have written elsewhere that I recently met a young undergraduate who startlingly claimed that 'We are all cartoonists now.'[10] She meant everybody, even those who cannot draw at all; she meant that we all now take the piss out of everything – even when we're not joking. We do not have to be able to draw to do it: we only need to be world-weary and cynical. Even pictograms are not required. In the 60s, we called piss-taking 'satire', but in those distant days we hoped for and expected a better world. Flowers were tucked into the barrels of guns, but the flowers died. The guns are still around. Today, satire – like gags – has suffered relegation. The cartoonist is still an observer of the life about him, but so is every Tom, Dick and Harry and every Alex, Sylvia and Patricia. Television has robbed the cartoonist of his readers. The computer offers markets of an uncertain nature in an uncertain future. The joke cartoonist has been dethroned – by change, by circumstances, by the very things the cartoonist used to laugh at. In the past he has always adapted to social and technological change. The challenge now is to adapt not only to a society but to a world which seeks its amusements elsewhere, and to a technology which offers too many alternatives.

References

1. I have excluded the Comic Creators' Guild because membership consists of comic-strip artists. Strips belong to a world distinct from cartooning and one that has a different, probably brighter, future in store.
2. See *Writers' & Artists' Yearbook 1996:* Classified index of markets for cartoons in newspapers and magazines. pp. 339, 340.
3. Information from Terry Christien, Secretary of the Cartoonists' Club of Great Britain and also Secretary of the Cartoonists' Guild.
4. E.H. Gombrich and E. Kris, *Caricature* (King Penguin, London, 1940), p. 1.
5. Ibid. p. 15.
6. *WittyWorld International Cartoon Magazine* No 17, Winter/Spring 1994 pp. 11, 12.
7. M. Dorothy George, *Hogarth to Cruikshank: Social Change in Graphic Art* (Allen Lane, London, 1967), p. 13.
8. Ibid.
9. The British Cartoonists' Association's Memorial Dinner for Carl Giles, OBE 1916-1995, Wynkyn de Worde, London, 26 October 1995.
10. John Jensen, 'The Mysterious Silence of Australian Cartoonists', BASA Conference paper, University of Kent at Canterbury, 1994.

Television was the killer of the gag cartoon – the slow poison of the hapless gag merchant...

Britain is no longer a comfortable, secure nation assured of its role in the world.

[1,2] John Jensen, *Spectator*, 5 May 1973; 16 February 1974

If desert islands, fakirs, monks, husbands-home-from-work, and rolling-pin-touting wives did not entirely disappear, they were no longer a major cartoon presence.

[3,4] John Jensen, *Daily Express*, 21 October 1958; undated.

'I agree, Miss Finch, it's not the gift, it's the thought behind it!'

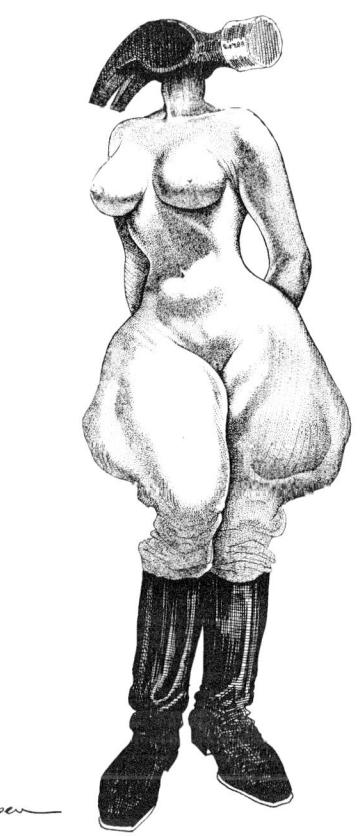

The girlie-gag, a staple of so many cartoons, rose from the coy he/she gags of the 1920s and earlier to the now boring secretary-on-Boss's knee jokes of the 1930s, 1940s and 1950s.

[5] John Jensen, *Quiz* (Australia), January 1950.

During the 1960s the girlie-gag was replaced by sterner images.

[6] John Jensen, 'Women's Lib', 1967. Private Collection.

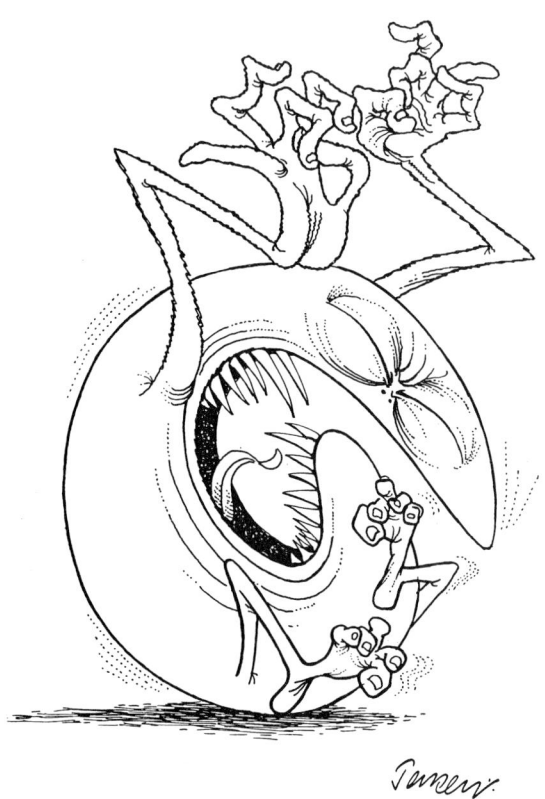

First published thirty-eight years ago – when people raged against The Bomb – today the image still holds good . . Road rage, office rage and domestic rage are everywhere.

[7] John Jensen, *Daily Express*, 16 September 1958.

People raging at everything around them will be in no mood for quiet, reflective chuckles which insist that everything is for the best of all possible worlds.

[8] John Jensen, *Goode's Magazine*, Vol.1, No.1, 1995.

It's No Laughing Matter to Some[1]
Ralph Steadman

Ever since grunting humankind stood up and made its first marks on cave walls, the cartoon has been a unique tool. Leonardo da Vinci regarded cartoons as working drawings for big ideas – not a bad description of shorthand lines which represent the outward expression of a thought; a kind of commonplace surrealism we have all learnt to read quickly. We have developed a highly sophisticated visual vocabulary to interpret what can be the simplest of messages, told with the fewest of lines which are as personal as handwriting. Within the last century there have been many artists who have spilled over into this vocabulary to express themselves to the fullest extent; to take a line for a walk, as Paul Klee is claimed to have said. Picasso and de Kooning are prime examples of painters who have in this century adopted a cartoonist's distorting characteristics to search the surface of their canvas for the irrational and the unexpected.

For more than a century, newspaper editors have recognised the value of cartoons, mainly because they help to sell newspapers. Yet, to this day, the cartoon remains a poor man's art, a dogsbody often seen as a space-filler; a last minute scribble that, in its humblest form, fills the gap left by someone who didn't file enough copy. In its humblest form it jockeys for a place somewhere between the crossword puzzle and the small ads. In its place of honour, next to the leader column, it serves as a readily digested pictorial version of the writer's elegiac wisdom for those who cannot read, for pictures attract those who do not wish to read, who cannot read, or who just will not understand. Cartoons represent a threat to writers – writers do not say so in so many words but they keep cartoons at arms' length. They merely use them to break up their acres of grey print, to titillate the eye rather than the mind. Cartoonists thus play a supportive role to the writer – or at least that is what those who commission them would like us to believe.

In contrast, the varying degrees of excellence in the cartoon form have crept upwards towards, and ultimately include, the greatest artists who ever lived. The cartoonist's impulse to express an idea simply is the root of all great art; but the device of the cartoon has also been used to escape the restrictive definitions of 'Art'. A cartoonist's line can convey humour, anger, sadness, wisdom, perception, sickness, poverty, pride, lust, greed, even a recognisable individual. Yet, put shoulder to shoulder next to a so-called work of fine art in a temple of art, the cartoon was still nothing more than a joke or even propaganda – a predetermined role that denied its due esteem as a work of art. Cartoonists represented a lowly profession, and it required artists such as Hogarth, Rowlandson, Gillray, Grandville, Daumier, Cruikshank and Goya to forge the cartoon into a weapon that did not command the approval of the Establishment. It flourished instead in the gutter along with actors, jugglers, and other sideshows to polite society. These artists were magnificent because they were uncompromising. They played the real game.

The political/social cartoon manifests itself in its purest form only when the need is greatest. During the Thirties in Germany, cartoonists and painters like George Grosz, Otto Dix, John Heartfield and Max Beckmann were forced to emigrate or face extermination. Their power to expose and lay bare fatuous lies and patent immoralities made their flight imperative. Interestingly, none of them seems to have been able to function as effectively outside the environment which fed their outrage.

In the late 60s, out of the Sorbonne student riots a Paris magazine was born called *L'Enragé*, 'The Enraged', which featured cartoon drawings exclusively. It survived only six issues but published some of the most wicked and perceptive insights into that period of history, intended to be digested at a glance. The cartoons were anarchic and a risk to any government. Today, however, the cartoon has become the politician's friend and ego-booster. If you haven't been drawn or sculpted by the best cartoonists around, you haven't arrived. Rather than attacking their subject, cartoonists pump energy into a public persona, turning all – well-meaning souls and villains alike – into light entertainment personalities. These politicians' policies, some of which have caused misery to thousands, are transformed into jolly, acceptable euphemisms for something we know in our hearts is wrong.

But if it does not feel uncomfortable, ridicule, and provide insight on an intellectual level, what is the cartoon's purpose? If it is not a corrective of some sort, it plays the politician's game and wallows in the realms of light entertainment. It must be said that the cartoon's purpose is not just to be funny. It is a sad fact, but oppression, deceit, and injustice are the mothers of satire, the cartoonist's best weapon. A satirist without a cause is a frustrated person.

Eight years ago, in a vain effort to help the cartoon avoid falling into this trap, I produced a 'manifesto' called 'Cabinet of the Mind', which demonstrated with examples how to portray a political type without drawing specific personalities. I urged all cartoonists worldwide to stop drawing politicians. I considered that if all cartoonists did that, even for one year, politicians as we knew them would change: if we denied them the benefit of our attention, insight and wit, they would suffer withdrawal symptoms of such withering magnitude that the effect on their egos could only be guessed at. Not even a tyrant can survive the whiplash of indifference. My plea appears to have fallen on deaf ears, but I have stuck to my resolve. I still occasionally draw politicians, but only their legs. It seems more insulting somehow.

God knows, right now, the world is in a bloody mess, and it confounds a body to know what to do to put it right. I do not think that cartoonists have the answer any more than some well-funded government department. It is a bloody world we live in, and we are stuck with it.

Reference

1. Extracts taken from *Observer Magazine*, December 1992, p. 7.

[9] Ralph Steadman; George Orwell, *Animal Farm: A Fairy Story* (Secker & Warburg, London, 1995).

I still occasionally draw politicians, but only their legs. It seems more insulting somehow.

[10] Ralph Steadman, *Observer Magazine*, December 1992, p. 30.

The political cartoon manifests itself in its purest form only when the need is greatest.

[11] Ralph Steadman, *Between the Eyes* (Jonathan Cape, London, 1984), p. 223.

Harold Wilson

[12] Ralph Steadman; *The Thoughts of Chairman Harold* (The Gnome Press, London, 1967).

Edward Heath

[13] Ralph Steadman; *Private Eye*, April 1968.

Margaret Thatcher

[14] Ralph Steadman, *Between the Eyes* (Jonathan Cape, London, 1984), p. 231.

One Thing After Another
Steve Bell

If Architecture is the mother of the Arts, then the Comic is the bastard single-parent grandmother. It is as old as the Human Race.

Political Comics are as old as Politics, which is roughly the same age as Morality and Religion. We do not know if palaeolithic cave paintings were intended as religious icons or as political cartoons. We can never know. All we do know is that meaning drains from an image over time, leaving us with the visual husk. Meaning also drains from an image over distance, which is why looking at foreign as well as ancient political cartoons can be an experience akin to looking at cave paintings.

When we 'read' images, our eyes are free to wander. Images have an autonomy that words do not. Words have to be read in sequence. Images can be read in sequence, but they don't have to be. The relationship between image and narrative is always semi-detached, they disrupt narrative as much as they contribute to it. One can intend to give a particular meaning to a sequence or juxtaposition of images, but this meaning is not necessarily what is delivered, because new meanings are created by the actual process. This is the language of montage, which is also the language of comics.

Anyone who works in the area of comics and cartoons in this country, where Literature dominates Culture, labours of necessity under a massive inferiority complex. Writers tend to occupy all the positions of power and responsibility. Meanwhile, our world is drowning in imagery. We receive more high-quality imagery in a fortnight's junk mail or five minutes' TV than the average 17th century peasant would see in an entire lifetime. We have a vocabulary of imagery that is growing apace, yet we have no language with which to articulate it. Those of us who labour in the field of image manipulation are regarded in the same light as a monstrous toddler with a loud noise at one end and no sense of responsibility at the other. In some ways it is worse than being patronised, the word 'cartoon' has become an all-purpose adjective to denote puerility, shoddiness, gross oversimplification and general unreality.

Photography suffers equally from a sense of inferiority; either used as space-filler, to 'look well on a page' amidst a sea of text, or kicked upstairs to the realm of Art. The poverty of our visual culture is well demonstrated by our newspapers. The 'tabloids' – the ones that look more like comics because of a greater apparent emphasis on imagery – are looked down upon. I would contend that most 'tabloids' are well worth looking down on, not because of their increased use of imagery, but because of their virulence and their stupidity. Most broadsheets are every bit as virulent and stupid as their tabloid counterparts; they simply do it at greater length which, in a culture that mistakes verbiage for thought, is more often than not regarded as sagacity.

The principle of reportage, of the freedom of comment and the sacred nature of fact, is still the principle by which most journalists justify their existence (no matter whether they are deluded or not). What is hard to understand is the misuse or non-use of photography in most journalistic endeavours. Why (other than in *Hello!*) are picture stories so rare? Why, when there are so many accomplished and experienced photojournalists around, is such a tiny fragment of their work ever made visible? One could argue that television has taken over the role of the photojournalist, were it not for the fact that the disdain for the use of imagery in the production of television news is probably even greater than that of print journalism.

Is it the fault of the image-makers that our culture is unable to cope with imagery? The *Sun* is often dismissed as a comic, which for someone who has always worked in the area, I regard as the profoundest personal insult. A comic is of essence a far more intelligent medium – both in its use of narrative and in its deployment of imagery – than a mere newspaper or magazine. Newspapers could be so much more interesting if they would learn a few lessons from comics about articulating images in a narrative form. What the *Sun* is in fact is a very centrally directed propaganda sheet where text is dominant. As in any other newspaper, photographs are used either as fillers or isolated 'events', which lead into the textual 'explanation'. In a proper comic the text is linked into the flow of imagery, and vice versa. Any flow of imagery in a newspaper is confined either to the comic section, or to those rare instances when a sequence of news photos is employed to record an actual event 'as it happened', and which usually involves someone falling off a high building.

Indeed, 'snuff' pictures are always regarded as the highest grade news, and this is by no means confined to the tabloids. I need only refer the reader to a book of news photographs selected by Harold Evans – former editor of the *Times* and the *Sunday Times* – entitled *Eyewitness*, which would have more accurately been entitled '101 Ways to Prematurely Shuffle Off This Mortal Coil'; and also to the front page of the *Independent* on the morning after the Lockerbie disaster; and then again after the Clapham railway smash. What intrigues me is the way such naively naked ghoulishness should be lauded as the highest quality journalism. What fascinates me still further is how the review pages of the same paper can take such a dismissive high moral tone in relation to the violence in the films of Quentin Tarantino.

Some of our less acute film critics have berated *Reservoir Dogs* and *Pulp Fiction* for being amoral and somehow making violence stylish. On the contrary, these films are tightly structured in the way comics are, and events are followed through with precisely the same relentless comic logic. The result is violence that truly shocks, that makes you sit up and feel ashamed of the fact that you are laughing, and yet which by the strength of the characterisation, pulls you back in and leads you on to the next absurd confrontation. The emphasis is always on cause and effect in human relationships; that if you shoot people it messes up your car, that death can be as entirely undramatic and as matter-of-fact as a sneeze. The sense of ironic dislocation induced by these films could be construed as amoral, but that is our problem. The technique is entirely moral.

The reason that actual 'snuff' pictures are regarded as such high-grade news is that (unlike a scene from the fictional *Reservoir Dogs*) they are such authoritative and arresting 'facts'. They have a definite rarity value, an unquestionable shock value, and – by having taken possession of an actual event – an unequalled voyeuristic appeal. Their use is very rarely morally justifiable. For me, the interesting thing about *Pulp Fiction* is that here at last we have a film that is striving to be a comic; not in any visual stylistic sense, but simply in the way it apprehends the reality that it is describing. It exists, as do comics, in the permanent present. As Tarantino says, in his films violence and stuff 'just happens'.

It is by now a commonplace to say that journalism is the first draft of history. If this is true of written journalism, then it must equally be true of photographed (and drawn) journalism. Why should such overriding importance be attached to 'as-it-actually-happened' snuff-type images, and so little significance be attached to visual storytelling or scene-setting? All films and photographs (no matter how fictional or fantastic) have a documentary role because, in the gnomic words of Jean-Luc Godard, they record 'Death at 24 frames a second'.

How do we come to terms with such power on the page? How do we marshal such hard, awkward, and uncontrollable 'facts' as news photographs into stories? History is a narrative we impose on events in retrospect. Each event can be viewed autonomously and can have a multitude of explanations. Sound historical practice will accommodate a diversity of sometimes contradictory explanations. Bad history will not 'let the facts get in the way of a good story'. The First Draft of Bad History might be an alternative title for the BBC's Birtian 'Mission to Explain'.

Television news is often dismissed as being too visual and too dependent on whatever striking imagery happens to have come in that day. In my opinion, television news is nowhere near visual enough. The 'Mission to Explain' cited above is in essence anti-visual. For me it is summed up by the talking head of Peter Jay being interviewed by the back of another talking head, and managing to explain in 600 words what a simple graph could explain in a millisecond. Walter Benjamin described photo-retouching as 'the bad artist's revenge on photography'. In many ways the 'Mission to Explain' is the bad journalist's revenge on television. Is it not time that TV journalism started working with the grain of imagery rather than against it? Might not that much maligned, apparently childish, yet highly sophisticated medium the comic have something to teach us here?

When Alfred Jarry stated that 'clichés are the armature of the absolute', from our present perspective he was being terribly profound. Cartoons are clichés by their very nature. They give us a hold on reality by simplifying it, while keeping it just about recognisable. They impart a tiny kind of power over a terrifying and incomprehensible world, which may in part explain why cave people drew elks on the wall.

We see the past through a veil of cliché and stereotype, both written and drawn. We see the French Revolution and George IV through Gillray. We see the history of the Irish rebellion through Gillray, Cruikshank and, less impressively, through JAK. We see the evils of drink in 18th- and 19th- century London through Hogarth and Cruikshank, and we see the underside of High Victorian London through Doré. But these images are more than stereotypes. They are lovingly obsessive records of a view of the world. Any political cartoon has to start with an opinion or a view. It is this which sustains the near lunatic amounts of energy needed to execute such works as the 'Worship of Bacchus' by George Cruikshank. The original painting is some 90 feet long and languishes in the bowels of the Tate Gallery. Some might argue that it is a Work of Art pure and simple, and that anyway it is not dealing with 'politics' as such, rather than with society in general. I would argue that it is a Work of Art with an ulterior motive, and this for me is the defining quality of a political cartoon.

A Work of Art without an ulterior motive is simply a Work of Art. It is about itself, its own material and its own methods. Some Works of Art develop the language of imagery and give us something to see with. Others do not.

The problem with the development of any visual language is the absence of an agreed structure. Since by definition such a language is beyond words, our only means of understanding it is subjective. We can only judge whether such a language works for us by reacting spontaneously to its effect on our eyeballs. This is why cartoonists keep referring back to existing imagery, to imagery which is so well known that it can provide a framework on which to hang other meanings, comments, cheap laughs or political obsessions. It is not just a desire to save effort (which it obviously does); instead it is a genuine attempt to establish some visual common ground.

Why do some images last? We can try to take them apart and see how they work by copying them. We can even copy them and interfere with them directly. We could write treatises on their iconography, on their formal composition, on the social history of the time of their creation, or on the psychic development of their creators. The History of Art was the history of hagiography, and has lately become the history of scientistic [sic] deconstruction. The imagery remains, and we can only keep looking at it and taking it apart. That is our sacred duty.

1.5 Excerpts from Steve Bell, 'A Psychopath, a Mega-nerd and Now Bambi', *Guardian*, 21 July 1994.

It took me several years before I realised that Margaret Thatcher was a psychopath. Conversely, it took less than a month to see that John Major was a mega-nerd. Margaret Thatcher definitely connived in her own depiction as the Iron Lady. It was an image she built for herself and played up to. The actual structure of her face took a long time to work out. It is largely to do with the angle of her nose in relation to her eyeballs, one of which is half-hooded, while the other swivels free. Once this is established, all else – the quiff, the neck, the pearls – falls into place.[1]

[15, 16, 17] Steve Bell, *Guardian*, 28 September 1995 (Methuen, London, 1987), p. 24; *Another Load of IF . . .*; *Maggie's Farm – The Last Roundup* (Methuen, London, 1981 5), p. 154.

I always found Kinnock impossible to draw, partly because he had the most difficult head, which seemed to change shape radically from every angle you looked at it. I was not helped by his lack of political definition and the strangulated foggy verbiage which characterised his journey rightwards.[2]

[18] Steve Bell, *Another Load of IF . . .* (Mandarin, London, 1984-5), p. 102;
The Vengeance of IF . . . (Mandarin, London, 1988-9), pp. 8-9.

The underpants are simply a metaphor for uselessness. I stumbled on them when, just after Major's accession to the leadership, I was looking at his record in office hitherto. It was a sorry tale of non-achievement, ranging from the cold-weather payments fiasco through to his ballsed-up entry into the ERM, so I drew him as a crap Superman. Superman wears sleek red briefs outside his tights; naturally John Major would wear Aertex Y-fronts outside his trousers. Only later did I hear the vile rumour as to where he tucks his shirt tails.[3]

[19] Steve Bell, *Guardian*, 19 December 1990 (first appearance of the underpants).

While Major has never connived in his depiction as a meganerd, he does play up to the image of plucky little ordinary chap, rather in the manner of Chaplin, or Hitler. He wears glasses, which for me always makes caricaturing easier because it is a ready-made structure on which you can build the likeness. Above all, he has a unique upper-lip structure, which, when I first drew him, tended to spread out in a ducklike manner until I saw a side view of him and realised that it swoops inwards and wraps itself around his front teeth. Add the weak chin poking out underneath and here you have him.[4]

Physically, Blair is more promising: teeth, ears, eyes and spiky hair are a sound basis for caricature, Politically, who knows? He's passionate about Europe; that's rather like being passionate about garden furniture. Along with everybody else on earth, apart from Margaret Thatcher, he believes in 'community' and the 'individual backed by the power of society', and he's a Christian. Some of my best friends are Christians. Maybe there's scope here for a few lion gags!⁵[5]

[20, 21] Steve Bell, *IF . . .Goes Down the John* (Methuen, London, 1991-2), p. 135; *Guardian*, 12 November 1993.

[22, 23] Steve Bell, *Guardian*, 9 January 1995; *Guardian*, 12 January 1996.

An Interview with Nicholas Garland [1]

John Harvey, 7 February 1994

I suppose the cartoon does, as an art form, have some sort of role. There is a great deal of hard news and thoughtful analysis in a newspaper, and it may be that to have a political cartoon which deals with the same news in another way is a good idea. The cartoon is a small space in which the news can be simplified, compacted and encapsulated, in a form which is comic or melodramatic or frivolous. It is all part of the orchestration of the paper. A paper isn't just the news, the sport, the features. You can think of it rather as like a story, with a beginning, a middle and an end; or as a symphony with different movements, one of which is where this funny thing happens, called a political cartoon. I think quite often people turn to the political cartoon just to get a change of mood and tempo, a kind of respite from the rest of the paper. Sometimes, perhaps, they even turn to it first of all, as a little *hors d'oeuvre* before anything else. But the time when political cartoons were used by the newspapers as a powerful, simple and easily understood expression of their own political views has long gone. A cartoon's significance now has more to do with the general arrangement of all the elements which make up a newspaper.

Cartoons have thus lost a great deal of their authority and power. This is partly because we are not such great artists as our predecessors. Earlier in this century there were people such as David Low, Leslie Illingworth, Vicky and Zec, for example. A number of others sometimes did political cartoons, even if they were not first and foremost political cartoonists. For instance, Bernard Partridge and Ernest Shepard did political cartoons in *Punch*. Even Giles did political cartoons during the Second World War – powerful drawings. Together, they were a fantastic line-up of talent. None of us is as good nowadays, I think. But it's very likely that if the cartoon were a more powerful and important feature, it would attract artists to itself. There are first-rate artists working in this country, but they are not so inclined to be political cartoonists: they work in strip cartoons, or books, or illustrations. Possibly fifty years ago they would have been drawn to the most important mode, which was political cartooning.

Of course there are some very good political cartoonists working nowadays. But the cartoon has to compete in the paper with photographs and very noisy, colourful advertisements. Even more important, there is television. People tend to turn to television for their information about the look and idiosyncrasies of politicians, rather than to cartoons. It is quite interesting, in the light of that, that probably the most well-known political cartooning these days is in *Spitting Image*, a TV programme and not a newspaper. We as cartoonists are very television-led, too. Because we have all been watching what has happened to Sarajevo, for example, we tend to think Sarajevo is some kind of unique hot-spot of horror. We forget that maybe fifteen thousand people have died in Armenia, or what has happened in the Horn of Africa. If you got a few TV cameras into Baku, or somewhere like that, everyone would start worrying about what was happening there. But if nobody's there, nobody is really reporting it. And I am like everybody else – I tend to follow where the news goes.

The themes of my cartoons come to me. I don't go looking for them. Political cartoonists need events, so I don't have favourite themes that I keep returning to. The majority of my cartoons are about British politics – the Tory Party, the Labour Party, the Foreign Office and foreign affairs. I am also concerned, of course, about international events – and there is something here about British politics which is striking. If you look at the political cartoons by Low or Vicky or Illingworth, particularly through the late 1930s to the early 1960s, you find that a large proportion dealt with foreign affairs. That includes the periods either side of the Second World War, obviously, so it is not surprising. But all through the 1950s, right up into the 1960s, there were major figures abroad who preoccupied us. John Foster Dulles, the American Secretary of State, was a very well known figure, compared with his recent successors. Or take President de Gaulle. Practically everything he did seemed to be major news over here, and we watched him very closely. The leaders of various other foreign countries were important figures to us too. But then came a time when we seemed almost exclusively involved with home matters – the strange decline of the Labour Party and the charismatic and extraordinary Prime Minister, Mrs Thatcher. With the fall of the Berlin Wall and the huge upheaval in eastern Europe and in the old Soviet Republics, the light began to shine on foreign affairs again. So I find that more and more of my cartoons now are suddenly to do with foreign affairs once more. There's another significant difference too. Right up until the 1960s we probably considered ourselves a world power. Therefore what we did abroad was naturally going to be reflected in our cartoons, because it mattered. But nobody believes we are in anything like that position now.

Reference

1. Interview conducted by John Harvey, Green College Oxford, 7 February 1994.

"JUST IGNORE THAT MOVE — IT'S ONLY ONE OF HIS PAWNS..."

All through the 1950s, right up into the 1960s, there were major figures abroad who preoccupied us.

[24] Vicky (Victor Weisz), *Evening Standard*, 28 November 1958.

Practically everything President de Gaulle did seemed to be major news over here, and we watched him very closely.

[25] Nicholas Garland, *Daily Telegraph*, 22 February 1967.

With the fall of the Berlin Wall . . .

[26] Nicholas Garland, *Independent*, 14 November 1989.

... and the huge upheaval in eastern Europe and in the old Soviet Republics, the light began to shine on foreign affairs again.

[27] Nicholas Garland, *Independent*, 24 November 1988.

One Genuinely Universal Bit of Mischief

Roger Law

The topical puppet show *Spitting Image* enjoyed a run of more than a decade on British television. This success resulted in a vast number of spin-offs, from best-selling comedy books to politician toby jugs and rubber dog-chews.

Some of the spin-offs that never made it were most bizarre. I remember a proposal from TV scientist Heinz Wolff that involved the puppets in a crazed idea, shooting nuclear waste into space. We passed on that one. There was also the condom book, featuring prophylactic politicians caricatured in latex. The book itself was a bellows: as you turned the page, up popped 'Johnny Major'. A prototype was ingeniously designed by my partner Peter Fluck. The publishers Faber & Faber were amazed at the book's ingenuity but the production costs proved prohibitive. It seems people will only pay so much for a joke.

Perhaps the most extraordinary aspect of the topical puppet show is its universality. Over the past few years similar shows have sprung up from Moscow to Tokyo, and it is this aspect that I find most intriguing.

The first approach was from the West Germans. They arrived at our East End Studios and wanted puppets made for a show they assured us would offend no one and would be in no way satirical. We said we thought those qualities were rather the point and after some debate we sent them back to West Germany to do their own thing. They did, and ironically the show they produced – entitled *Gum* – did indeed acquire a cutting edge. I saw a pastiche of the German movie *Das Boot*, with the entire German government sitting in a U-Boat being depth-charged. It was very effective.

The Italians came next. *Spitting Image* made puppets of the entire Italian government, sent them to Italy, and the Italian production team wrote and produced the show *Teste di Gomma*. On the morning of the day the show was to premiére, the entire Italian government resigned. Not good news for our Italian colleagues. We rang them up to commiserate, only to be told not to worry. The politicians 'would just re-shuffle and take different jobs – no problemo'.

The next arrival was a lone Hungarian, who wanted to make a show in Budapest. He had a great deal of determination but no money. I showed him all the processes by which the British show was made, and he went back to Budapest and eventually made a very successful Hungarian version on a shoe-string budget. I visited his studios in central Budapest and was taken aback by the ingenuity the penniless production team had brought to the show. He had told me over the phone that he had no money for sets, but his show-reel revealed the most extraordinarily elaborate set of the interior of the Hungarian Houses of Parliament. When I pointed this out, he told me they filmed all of the topicals in the actual Houses of Parliament. There was some remarkable filming done by balancing the puppeteers on skateboards using a hand-held camera – something we had never tried ourselves. The show, *Uborka*, was well received and mildly satirical. The producer said to me 'You British have been cutting the grass for over 400 years. We Hungarians have only been doing it for four.' The show played all winter and came off in the summer, and I asked him if there was any particular reason for this. He said: 'Yes – the caricaturist spends the summer in Hösök Tere (the main Square), drawing the tourists, where he earns more money.'

The Russians. Our initial contact was a Tartar by birth and a Tartar by nature. Tall and striking with perfect English, she was utterly autocratic, bullying the financial director and myself into travelling to Moscow for a series of meetings with a newly independent production company called 'Authors TV' (ATV). We arrived in Moscow during Yeltsin's honeymoon with the Russian people. No one seemed to be in control. The Russian producer and his colleagues negotiated for several days before a semblance of a deal could be put together. We agreed to teach the Russians how to make the puppets and the show. It would be called *Rubber Souls*, a play on the title of Gogol's book *Dead Souls*, and in return the Russians agreed to form a company of which 25 per cent belonged to *Spitting Image*. On our return to London, our managing director unkindly described the deal as '25 per cent of nothing'. Three years later we have yet to prove her wrong. During those years, the Russians have visited the London workshops for training, a visit which culminated in a farewell supper. Speeches were made and tears were shed. The Russian head writer told an involved joke about a family of worms living on a dung heap, the gist of which was that they had aspirations to live on the dung heap opposite. Not to be outdone, one of the British writers told the joke: 'What's the difference between your mother and a terrorist?' No one knew. 'You can negotiate with a terrorist.' 'What do you mean – my mother?' shouted one of the offended Russians. The British writer back-pedalled: 'Oh gosh, erm, not *your* mother, any mother, don't you see...'. In the end the Russian did see.

Together we toasted the British joke. Some months later, I received an encouraging fax from Moscow to say that the *Rubber Souls* team had made a New Year's Eve special, to be sent out to the 19 republics. On the night of the broadcast, however, they were told by the TV controller that it was not a good time to laugh at Boris Yeltsin. The New Year's Eve special remained on the shelf.

The first I had heard of the Bulgarian satire show *Coo Coo* was a phone call from *Private Eye*. Had I time to meet the producer from Bulgaria? Sure, I said. It transpired that she did not want a franchise, for the Bulgarians already had *Coo Coo*, a satire show with one puppet. Tapes were made available and we sat down to watch them. A news reporter appeared on screen outside the Bulgarian Houses of Parliament. As eminent MPs left, the news reporter introduced himself, said he was from Utamba in Africa, and asked if they would like to comment on the situation there. Each politician subsequently gave a detailed exposition of his party's position on Utamba. The news reporter then came very close to the camera and confided that he was in fact an exchange student from Zimbabwe and that Utamba did not exist. This routine was then followed by a vigorous interview with a military police guard outside a nuclear power station. 'Tell me', asked the young reporter, 'is it true that you have a meltdown inside the power station?' The military policeman looked terrified and his denials were none too convincing. This particular item, our producer told me with a grin, had caused a panic across Bulgaria and Romania – roads were blocked with fleeing cars, rather like Orson Welles' radio broadcast *War of the Worlds*. Our Bulgarian producer returned home. I thought perhaps we should go with her for lessons.

The Greeks came bearing cheques and a deal was struck. I visited their studios, an otherwise derelict warehouse, located in a suburb of Athens next to a huge olive-oil processing plant and a sluggish slick of evil-smelling pollution which might have been a river. The Greek puppeteers were puppeteers by day and security guards by night. The show was, I believe, 90 per cent political, with very good ratings. The first transmission was hampered by the government, who called a snap election and lost it to Andreas Papandreou. Unfortunately, all the puppets were caricatures of the previous administration. Unperturbed, the Greek writers put together a show revealing what the previous government would have done had they won the election and stayed in office. No lack of ingenuity in Athens.

A young energetic entrepreneur from Prague arrived at our London studios and told me that the first time he saw a tape of *Spitting Image* he vowed to make a similar show in the Czech republic, once the Communist regime crumbled – which he did. He agreed terms that day and we made arrangements for his team to come to London for training. I pointed out that the week he had allocated for his team's visit coincided with another potential visit by our Russians. The Czech roared with laughter and said, 'We put up with the Russians for 40 years – what's a few days more?' The Russians failed to turn up but the Czechs arrived.

The Czech show, *Gumaci*, was made in an old cinema in the gypsy quarter of Prague, put together by a very small team of hard-working professionals. They occasionally received a call from Mr Havel's new friends in Prague Castle, who pointed out that it is not a good idea to portray him as stupid since he most decidedly is not. *Gumaci* was well shot, imaginatively lit, and appeared to be satirical. It kept the sketches short and had energy. The team enjoyed making the show and were intent on improving standards week by week. Morale was high and so were the ratings. *Gumaci* was the third most successful show in the Czech Republic. I was amused to notice they have even picked up on one of our trade secrets, which is: when short of material, run a weatherman sketch.

I've not been to Japan to see the results of our Tokyo franchise. One of the *Spitting Image* directors did go over to teach the Nippon team the tricks of the trade and brought back videotapes of how the show is made, including interviews with the Japanese programme-makers and a short interview with Murray Sayle, a legendary Australian journalist who lives in Tokyo and writes about Japanese politics. Murray maintained the time was right for a Japanese *Spitting Image*, as never before had so much sincerity been shown by Japanese politicians – 'showing sincerity' being a euphemism for money changing hands. Certainly no shortage of material in Japan. In the Japanese tapes there was no noticeable 'going for the jugular', but the production itself was a lesson to us all. It was most extraordinary watching the puppeteers working in harmony and anticipating each other's moves. The tape of their very first show was more professional than anything we achieved in our first year.

When Peter Fluck and I worked a millennium ago on the pilot of the British show, we were asked if we thought it would be a success. Peter thought it might be a cult success, but I thought it would either die a quick death or be very successful, since I did not think it was the kind of idea or show that people could be neutral over. It was not going to be the kind of TV that washes over you from the corner of the room like warmth from an electric fire. Neither of us thought it would catch on anywhere else in the world except, perhaps, America. In the event, interest in the US has been more limited than elsewhere, though we have done a number of shows for the major networks there.

Despite our early reservations, we now hope to take TV franchises to the Brazilians, Argentinians, and South Africans, nor forgetting the Turks. It appears that the one bit of mischief genuinely universal in this world is taking the piss out of politicians on TV.

Roger Law and Peter Fluck: artisans

[28] Roger Law, *A Nasty Piece of Work* (Booth-Clibborn Editions, London, 1992) p. 147.

The success of *Spitting Image* has resulted in a vast number of spin-offs, from best-selling comedy books to politician toby jugs and rubber dog-chews.

[29] *The Appallingly Disrespectful Spitting Image Book* (Spitting Image Productions, London, 1985), and 'Thatchers' Toby Jug caricature sketch, from *A Nasty Piece of Work* (Booth-Clibborn Editions, London, 1992) p. 219.

Mrs. Thatcher carving up the Roast Beef of England – or 'The Plum-pudding in Danger' after Gillray.

[30] *Spitting Image*, from *The Cutting Edge* (Barbican Art Gallery Editions, London, 1992), p. 12.

Puppet heads of various sizes and materials on parade.

[31] Roger Law, *A Nasty Piece of Work* (Booth-Clibborn Editions, London, 1992), pp. 177, 219.

Drawings by *Spitting Image*'s head caricaturist, Pablo Bach.

[32] Roger Law, *A Nasty Piece of Work* (Booth-Clibborn Editions, London, 1992), pp. 208-9.

Editorial Cartoons: A Transatlantic Perspective

Kevin Kallaugher

As I see it, the fundamental feature which defines the differences between British and American cartooning lies in the contrasting geographies of the two countries. Britain is a relatively small country whereas America is a vast expanse of a continent, dotted with large and small metropolitan areas with individual populations ranging from 100,000 to several million. Each of these urban enclaves is serviced with one or at most two daily newspapers.

These differences in geography have fostered different working environments for the editorial cartoonists. London is a dynamic international hub. To work in London is to work in the centre of England's political power, its financial centre, and the home of its entertainment industry. To an American cartoonist, that would be like living in a city with the White House, Wall Street and Hollywood all within easy walking distance. Hence with such a concentration of wealth and power in one place there is never a dearth of material on which to comment, and as a result London maintains a healthy population of cartoonists whose works grace the numerous publications.

Each of the nine or ten national daily papers based in London will have its own editorial cartoonist. But most will also have several other cartoonists doing topical commentary work. There will be a pocket cartoonist on the front doing a small gag on the subject of the day, and there will be another cartoonist on the business pages covering financial stories in a gag or a strip format. There will be a caricaturist and other illustrators on the commentary and arts pages and a couple of comic strips nestled in strategic locations. A great many British cartoonists are freelance. They work for a variety of publications, each with a fixed arrangement. For example, in 1987 I was contributing four political cartoons a week to *Today*, one cartoon a week to the *Sunday Telegraph* and two caricatures a week to *The Economist*.

When I was in London, I found it a great advantage to open up the papers and discover what my opposite numbers in other papers were drawing on the same subject. Each cartoonist knew that the others were going to scour his/her work, and this set up a fraternal sense of competition which pushed each of us to strive to excel. Knowing that your colleague was looking over your shoulder meant you tried to avoid the obvious ideas and common clichés. It forced one to dig a little deeper for inspiration.

America is a fertile ground for cartoonists too, but its roots are very different from those of its transatlantic cousins. In the United States over 125 editorial cartoonists are employed on a full-time basis by newspapers and periodicals, and another 100 may do it on a part-time basis. However, this number hides the isolation which marks the trade in this country. As I mentioned before, the newspapers are highly regionalised. Each metropolitan area usually supports a single newspaper, working with a smaller market than in Britain. For instance, a large-circulation daily may get a readership of 300,000 from a population of 2 million. This compares to a 1 to 4 million circulation for some of the larger London newspapers with a nationwide audience.

Although the average American paper only employs one cartoonist, you will find other cartoons appearing in the newspaper. In fact, the average American paper seems to carry about 40 cartoons, mostly in the form of comic strips. However, these – like most of the artwork in the papers – are supplied by syndicates. Syndicates are wholesale distributors of newspaper features – cartoons, columnists, crosswords – who make their money by selling the product cheap to a mass market. It works like this: a cartoonist is taken on in New York by a syndicate who agrees to sell his/her work. The syndicate sends out brochures and salesmen to pursue the 1000-plus possible cartoon outlets. Subscribers are billed on a scale roughly proportional to their publication's circulation (circulation 1 million = $100 per week, circulation 100,000 = $20 per week). The gross revenue accumulated by the sales throughout the country is then divided between the syndicate and the syndicatee. The subscribing papers are happy because they can get a top cartoonist/columnist/crossword on their pages for a fraction of the price they would pay for a staff member. The syndicatee is happy because the potential for earnings is much higher than that earned working on a sole newspaper. But the poor cartoonist working for the *Memphis Commercial Appeal* is not happy at all; the syndicates have replaced all his cartoon colleagues! The poor fellow is alone and isolated.

Despite the insular nature of American cartooning, there is a very positive aspect to working as an editorial cartoonist in the USA. This is the 'power' which the cartoonist wields in his society. America on the whole has a very low level of satire, particularly political satire. In comparison to London, American cities do not have the same tradition of lampooning their leaders on TV, radio and in print, except in the editorial cartoon. Therefore, without much competition in the satire stakes, American cartoonists stand out as beacons of irreverence. A great deal of attention is brought to bear on the cartoonist because of this.

In the first place, politicians take great notice of, and are very sensitive to, the fluctuations in voters' opinions. American politicians – by constantly surveying the polls – try desperately hard to create a positive 'spin' on their every action. As television is the *modus operandi* of communication in America, politicians toil hard to control their image through well chosen soundbites, and well crafted TV images of themselves. Who in their community can explode their myth to a massive audience? The cartoonist, of course! In many cities around the country, the resident cartoonist is considered Public Enemy No.1 by Governors in the state capitals – and these are not just minor politicians. In the American form of devolved government, state politicians hold tremendous power (the state of California has a population of 70 million); Bill Clinton, Ronald Reagan and Jimmy Carter were all state governors before they became President.

Also paying close attention to the work of the cartoonists are the readers. Since each US metropolitan area has but one daily newspaper, these areas have no choice but to read it. This one publication must serve the community, which runs the full gamut of the socio-political spectrum, from up-market conservatives to down market lefties. As you can imagine, it is very difficult for editors, try as they may, to please such a variety. For a cartoonist, it is an impossible task. Each and every cartoon ticks somebody off. The readers, angry that they have no choice but to ingest an opinion contrary to their own, let their feelings be known to the paper. The cartoonist, as a result, is the recipient of a great deal of hate mail, and even death threats. The high visibility of the cartoonist makes him/her a lightning rod for criticism. But being at the centre of controversy also gives the local cartoonist a sense of notoriety. Americans, since the days of Bonnie and Clyde, have long confused fame and notoriety, so being the local bad boy/girl actually adds some cachet to the cartoonist's status.

This reaction from American politicians and readers to editorial cartoons is, in my view, significantly different from that found in Britain. In London each of the dailies and weeklies has carved out its own particular niche. For example, at one end of the spectrum the *Daily Telegraph* aspires to a Conservative, middle-class readership, and at the other end the *Mirror* looks towards a more working-class Labour supporter. So distinct is the readership of the British press, that if you gaze around the carriage on the 9.53am semi-fast Brighton to London train, you could quite accurately learn a lot about your fellow passengers just by observing what newspaper they chose to buy.

British politicians do not seem to take the same notice of cartoonists as do their American counterparts. Perhaps they do not believe that cartoonists have the power they once had to change public opinion. Or perhaps with so much other satire on television, radio and in print the cartoonists are just an amusing sideshow. Recently the Republican Congressional Leader Newt Gingrich tried to ban an Atlanta newspaper from having any access to Congress because he claimed they had printed an objectionable cartoon. I am sure many British cartoonists wish their politicians were as easily roused by cartoons as it seems the American politicians are!

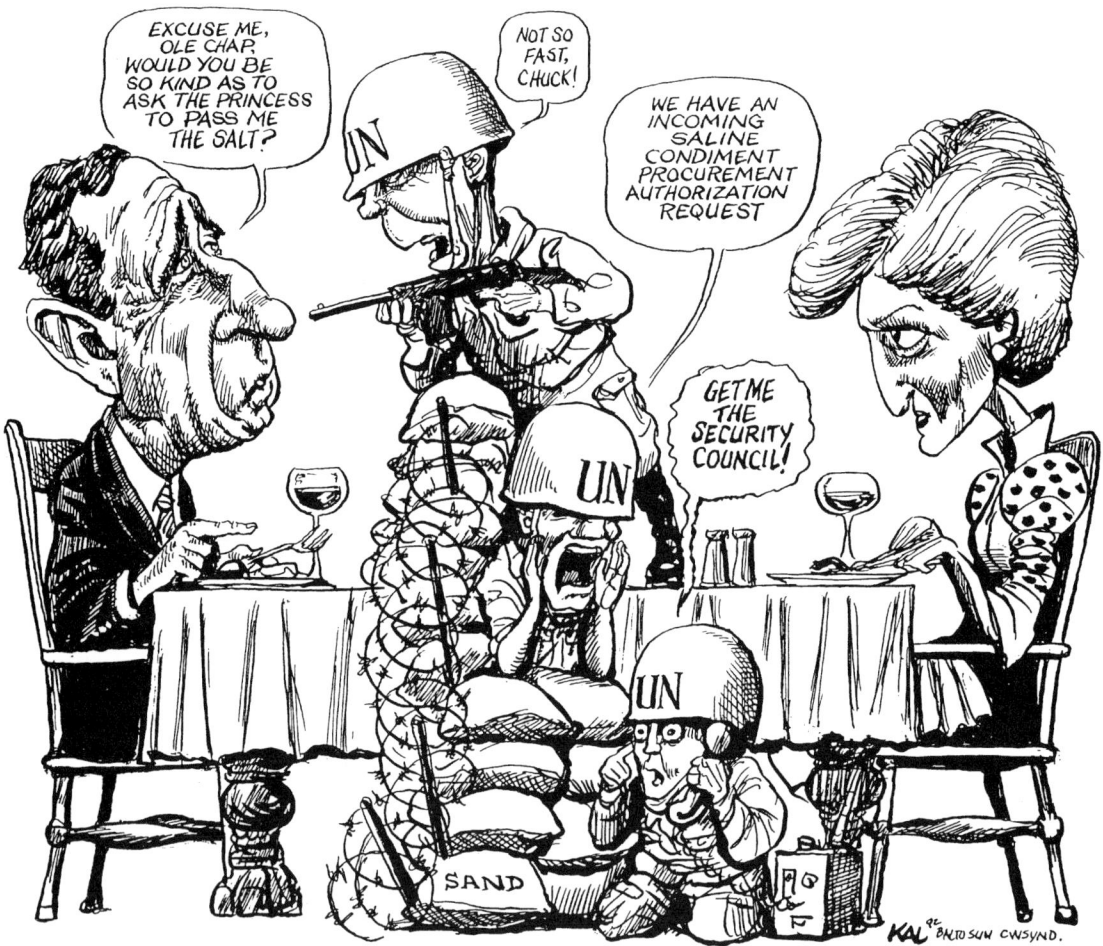

[33] KAL, *Baltimore Sun*/Creators and Writers' Syndicate, 1992.

[34] KAL, *Baltimore Sun*/Creators and Writers' Syndicate, 1993.

[35] KAL, *Baltimore Sun*/Creators and Writers' Syndicate, 2 May 1993.

Poison Pen or Good-Tempered Pencil?
Humour and Hatred in 20th Century Political Cartoons

Mark Bryant

Rutherford had once been a famous caricaturist, whose brutal cartoons had helped to inflame popular opinion before and during the revolution.

George Orwell, *Nineteen Eighty-Four*.[1]

In Orwell's dystopic vision of the future, the all-powerful ruler Big Brother only allows three of his original fellow-revolutionaries to survive the subsequent purges and it is no accident that one of these, Rutherford, is a political cartoonist. Like the real-life leaders of the totalitarian regimes satirised in the book, Big Brother is only too aware of the power of the political cartoon to excite the emotions and to reach the soul of the masses in the most immediate way possible. As Hitler himself said in *Mein Kampf*: 'At one stroke... people will understand a pictorial presentation of something which it would take them a long and laborious effort of reading to understand.'[2] A picture, indeed, does paint a thousand words, but as James Cameron once said, it does rather depend on who draws the pictures and who writes the words.

But what type of cartoon drawing is the most effective? The novelist John Fowles in his essay 'Remembering Cruikshank' identifies the 'essential weakness' of one of Britain's acutest graphic satirists as being 'too much humour, not enough anger – a very English combination'.[3] It is a tradition that has continued through the 19th century and into the 20th. We recall Fougasse's dictum of always using a 'good-tempered pencil'[4] in order to hit the target. But then again Fougasse was primarily a social commentator – not a political cartoonist – and, as the only cartoonist to be editor of *Punch*, he was both a product of as well as a contributor to that magazine's rather genteel stance on 'picture-politics'. However, even this country's first staff political cartoonist, Sir Francis Carruthers Gould, confessed in similar vein that 'I etch with vinegar, not vitriol'[5] and the great humorist Ambrose Bierce declared that 'The only person pained by an offensive cartoon is its author; the only person pained by a ridiculous one is its victim.'[6] Even the admirable Sir David Low, no shrinking violet when it came to attacking politicians or wartime dictators, always did so – and very deliberately – with a sense of levity. His humour may sometimes have been a dark shade of grey but it was never completely black. As he himself says, ridicule is always the best weapon – malice rarely succeeds: 'It clouds the judgement.'[7]

But is this really the case? Sir Ernst Gombrich has commented that 'In fact, the satirists' attempts to turn monsters into figures of fun have usually misfired.'[8] And even in domestic politics this has often held true – one only has to think of Vicky's creation of 'Supermac' or the Russians' christening of Margaret Thatcher as 'the Iron Lady'. What, after all, is wrong with malice? In his essay on 'Comic Art' in *English Humour*, J.B. Priestley goes further and sees this as the defining aspect of a classic political cartoonist of an earlier generation to Cruikshank – James Gillray:

> What distinguishes him, apart from his magnificent technique, is a malice at once so shrewd and passionate that it has a touch of sublimity about it. It was a bad day's work for George III when he made a lasting enemy of Gillray... never was any man, king or commoner, handled with more devastating malice.[9]

In similar vein, the power of the 'ugly' political cartoon in both war and peace in the 20th century has been undeniable – both at the time of first publication and to anyone looking back now. From the gruesome anti-Kaiser pictures of Louis Raemakers and Edmund Sullivan to those of the Nazi-hating Soviet 'Kukryniksi' trio (Kupryanov, Krylov and Sokolov), and from the virulent anti-Semitic work of the contributors to *Der Stürmer* to Dyson's bloated capitalists and the ghoulish figures which feature in what is known as Vicky's 'Oxfam' style. These are pictures expressing extremes of negative emotion – of anger and hatred, of pain and disgust – drawn by people of commitment who, like Goya, like George Grosz, like the photo-montage artist John Heartfield, have something terrible to say and do so in the most poignant way possible. John Berger draws a parallel between Gerald Scarfe and Gillray, Goya and Daumier: 'what is essential to them is that they draw faithfully – and with pain – the ghosts that crowd in on them'.[10] Yet what they are drawing are still cartoons and very fine ones at that.

But, it might be argued, perhaps these shouldn't be called cartoons at all? Surely it is in the definition of a cartoon to be funny in some albeit distant or perhaps wry way? This certainly seems to be the public perception – rightly or wrongly. Some year's ago when working on a book called *World War II in Cartoons*, a friend turned on me for seeming to trivialise or joke about a frightful business; I was made to feel that I had committed some ghastly *faux pas*. When the book eventually appeared all was forgiven, of course – a single glance showed that these were not comic fripperies. To be sure, many of the cartoons were indeed funny, of the kind Kenneth Bird has characterised as 'humour under pressure', but equally many were quite the opposite. Cartoonists, after all, are people, and like anybody else, react to situations in differing ways. Nervous types often giggle; others may cry with happiness. When Henry VIII first appeared with his despised new queen, Anne Boleyn, their clothes were decorated with their entwined initials and the mob laughed at the lettering, 'HA HA HA' – but without any humour or warmth. And in wartime in particular, the 'pressure' on cartoonists can be so great that the element of humour may disappear altogether in their portrayal of events.

This confusion about the place of humour in visual satire seems to continue in some people's minds with regard to contemporary political cartoons. In 1992 for example, MAC of the *Daily Mail* received a letter from an outraged inhabitant of the Home Counties when he drew a cartoon attacking the action of snipers shooting children in former Yugoslavia. The writer – who had obviously completely misunderstood the cartoon, as it was neither visually funny nor had a humorous caption – accused him of making a joke out of a deeply upsetting incident. He was evidently also not a regular *Mail* reader, otherwise he would have known that MAC usually includes a hidden portrait of his wife in his humorous cartoons, but deliberately omits it in the more serious ones.

The assumption that all cartoons are necessarily funny or at least contain an element of humour thus does seem to persist. Unfortunately, however, we are stuck with the word and its many very different shades of meaning, from animation to continuity strip, from single joke to the blackest of political drawings – and even, of course, its original pre-Leech sense of an artist's template. 'Caricature' would be a helpful alternative but increasingly these days in Britain the word is only used to denote portrait caricature – which is just one element in the political cartoonist's armoury.

The danger is that the label 'cartoonist', with its bubblegum-and-freckles image, also thereby seems to imply that the artist himself is equally inconsequential and lightweight. This would be grossly unfair to cartoonists in general, but it is doubly so to the political cartoonist. After all, to survive – let alone succeed – in this immensely stressful profession, the political cartoonist has to sit down each day with a blank sheet of paper, absorb every aspect of the day's news, produce anything up to six roughs by mid-morning and then create a cartoon which is topical, well drawn, features recognisable caricatures of leading celebrities, is in some indefinable but powerful sense 'telling', and also, if possible, is spiced (but not necessarily so) with some large grains of wry humour. But the most important thing is always the message – without that it fails completely. As the Dutch cartoonist Fritz Behrendt has said, 'The political cartoonist is a close relative of schoolmasters, missionaries, prophets and moralists: and his primary aim is not belly laughter, but the thoughtful smile which shows that the graphic signals have been understood.'[11] It is a 'knowing' smile – if it is there at all – and not a happy one. And an immense amount of effort – both in skilled draughtsmanship and heartfelt political commitment – goes into each and every drawing (there is, as someone once said, no such thing as an unsigned political cartoon). These are people worthy of our respect.

Typically, the cartoonists themselves make light of their current lowly status. In MAC's office at the *Daily Mail* hangs a drawing by Kliban in which an insignificant-looking man, locked arm-in-arm with two glamorous escorts, walks down a city street as a uniformed guard pushes people aside. 'Out of the way, you swine!' the caption reads, 'a CARTOONIST is coming!' However, not everybody, it would seem, sees things this way. Even amongst the closely knit professional community itself there are notes of discord. The distinguished cartoonist Bill Tidy no doubt appreciates the above sentiment generally, but he evidently does not think it applies to political cartoonists. In his autobiography he writes:

> political cartoons were of no interest to me. I considered them... and still do, the easiest and most predictable facet of the trade. The situations are presented on a plate, editors insist that the end product is overdrawn to fit a large space, and usually such cartoons serve exactly the opposite purpose to what was intended – they please politicians so much that they write and ask for the original![12]

The latter statement reinforces Gombrich's point, but it is significant that – according to Kenneth Baker at least[13] – politicians normally only buy *flattering* portraits of themselves. Which further strengthens the argument in favour of the 'ugly' political cartoon – rather than a humorous one – being a more effective way of attacking an individual. The rest of Tidy's opinions of political cartoonists seem to me unfair, particularly regarding contemporary artists, though no doubt there may have been some of his acquaintance to whom these comments might have applied in the past.

Kenneth Baker has also pointed out that, ironically, 'politicians need cartoonists, for to be caricatured is a sign that they have arrived' – a strange symbiotic relationship indeed. So much so, in fact, that the 'tabs of identity', as Low calls them, by which a cartoonist establishes a visual shorthand for his target, can even be invented by the politician himself for use by both cartoonists and stand-up comedians/impressionists alike. A well-known case in point is Harold Wilson's pipe; in private he actually preferred cigars. But it should be stressed that this inter-relationship does not always work out the way the politicians expect. Adolf Hitler, for example, once allowed an exhibition to be held featuring the work of anti-Nazi cartoonists. This, he presumably hoped, would prove how 'big' he had become – as Colin Seymour-Ure says in *The Political Impact of Mass Media* (talking of the role of *Private Eye* in Britain), 'by tolerating the Fool the King shows his own strength'.[14] Unfortunately for Hitler, it appears that he too fell into the trap of thinking that cartoons were necessarily funny (as did his fellow dictator, Mussolini, who was apparently a great fan of Donald Duck). In the event, many of the drawings were so savage that the show had to be closed down – proving once again the power of the odious as opposed to the humorous cartoon. Some Kings have been even less tolerant of their Fools. Daumier was imprisoned for six months for a single cartoon attacking Louis Philippe. Thomas Theodor Heine suffered the same fate at the hands of Kaiser Wilhelm, and in London in 1987 the Lebanese political cartoonist Naji al Ali was shot dead by his countrymen for his activities. No laughing matter.

The political cartoonist is an important person. He is not an entertainer or soft-centred pedlar of jokes. He is no Fool, nor is he a fool. The cartoonist John Jensen has said that 'satire without purpose is mere derision'.[15] Quite so. And by the same token the political cartoonist is not by definition or even primarily in the business of humour. He is a crusading journalist who is able to express him- or herself better than anyone else on the publication he works for, simply because he does not need words. And those who do not need words, do not need language, which means that they are able to reach infinitely further than conventional text-chained commentators, taking their message to the deaf, the illiterate and – perhaps most important of all – to the countless millions who have a different mother tongue. At the British Cartoonists' Association's 25th anniversary dinner, Mel Calman took issue with guest speaker Miles Kington for being 'merely' a writer: 'Anyone can write,' Calman said, 'it's drawing that's difficult.' And, he might have added, drawing with purpose is tougher still.

It has been said that in producing ugly cartoons you thereby produce an ugly newspaper, and people don't buy ugly things. This seems almost as ludicrous as to say that a canvas is sullied by the artist's paint. Low and Vicky both worked for Lord Beaverbrook in total opposition to the political standpoint of the papers they contributed to, but this did not stop sales. Scarfe's anti-Vietnam, anti-Nixon grotesqueries were not only a talking point in the *Sunday Times* of the period but ironically are now fabulously expensive to buy in contrast to the drawings of many other cartoonists working at that time and making the same political points. But they certainly are not pleasant to look at, nor were they ever meant to be. These are not lampoons but vicious personal attacks, redolent of venom and bile. As Scarfe himself has said: 'My drawings are often a cry against that which I detest, and in showing my dislike I have to draw the dislikeable.'[12] If you are in the business of news then your duty is to show it all, and bad news – as witness the Rosemary West murder trial – can often be good for sales.

Editors, of course, occasionally do suppress drawings they think go too far (Vicky produced a whole book of such rejections)[16], but fewer cartoons are 'spiked' in this way than people might think. Nicholas Garland usually only cites one (Maggie as the Iron Lady with her knickers falling down) and Steve Bell – after many years on the *Guardian* – had his first in November 1995 (featuring John Major as a talking turd). The political cartoonist, after all, has to be allowed to make his personal statement. But it is more often than not the bad-taste 'funny' cartoon that is dropped rather than the 'ugly' one. There is humour and horror, but to laugh at something tragic is beyond the pale. The sort of person who *enjoys* 'snuff movies', is in very real terms, sick. But this is where the confusion persists. The political cartoonist is not by definition making a joke out of everything he draws. What he is doing is making a comment; sometimes it is funny, sometimes it is ironical, satirical, witty, mocking. But at another times it is simply ghastly, and the message cannot be communicated in any other way.

David Low admired Cruikshank as a 'clown in white gloves' yet was uncomfortable with his more brutal work. But as V.S. Pritchett – coincidentally the grandfather of the *Daily Telegraph*'s popular pocket cartoonist, Matt – has said, 'Low lacks the morbid genius of hatred.'[17] And there is a long tradition in this country of bare-knuckle satire, of cartooning, as it were, with the white gloves off. The vibrant, salacious and often cruel lampoons of the 18th century caricaturists contributed to the downfall of at least one Prime Minister, Lord Bute, and did great damage to many other politicians, as well as the royal family, in a time of unprecedented sleaze and corruption. In their drawings, Gillray, Rowlandson and others certainly didn't mince words. And their function above all was to make the public think for itself. To return to Pritchett:

> And here is the danger; a great deal of the high-minded disapproval of unkindness or irreverence in satire springs from anger at being asked to think again. Far worse, we are angry with the satirist for

threatening our contemporary sense of security. In a democracy, a cartoonist teaches people to think for themselves...

... and sometimes we have to think unpleasant things. And frequently the best way to communicate this is with an ugly drawing. Ambrose Bierce, in criticising this approach, said: 'We like to laugh, but we do not like – pardon me – to retch.' True, but if retching is the only way to combat poison then it is sometimes necessary to allow the political cartoonist to stick his artistic fingers down society's throat.

In Orwell's bleak book, Rutherford is spotted by Winston Smith in a café, a crushed and defeated man, his cartoons

> simply an imitation of his earlier manners and curiously lifeless and unconvincing... At one time he must have been immensely strong; now his great body was sagging, sloping, bulging, falling away in every direction. He seemed to be breaking up before one's eyes, like a mountain crumbling.

Rutherford, sadly, had succumbed to the system. But the system here, be it remembered, is no longer a democracy, but a totalitarian state administered by the dreaded Thought Police.

Britain has a proud tradition both in democratic politics and vigorous cartooning, going back to the days of Hogarth, but unfortunately in recent years the image of the cartoon has faltered. Indeed, 'The term "cartoonist" has been so enfeebled by the countless numbers who have drawn purely for humorous effect that there has almost been lost all sense of his real identity' (Behrendt).

The role of the political cartoon is of immense importance in a democracy and in order to fulfil this function humour may often have to be discarded in the interests of Truth. Cartooning has been called 'the art of laughter'. This may still hold true of Disney, 'Peanuts' and 'Garfield' but for the political cartoonist it is, and always has been, a deeply serious business. And it is often far from easy – let alone desirable – to get one's message across in a humorous way. Vicky believed that a cartoon was a signed statement of principles, and the medium of newsprint – with its stark contrast of ink on white paper – is perfectly suited to making direct statements of this kind. Colour, of course, also has its advantages in attacking the ogres of injustice, red in tooth and claw, but whether the ink is monochrome or rainbow-hued, the most effective political cartoons have often, undeniably, been very, very black.

References

1. George Orwell, *Nineteen Eighty-Four* (Secker & Warburg, Collected Works Edition, 1987), pp. 79-80.
2. Adolf Hitler, *Mein Kampf*, Book II, Chapter VI (Hutchinson, 1969).
3. John Fowles, 'Remembering Cruikshank' in Mark Bryant (ed.) *The Comic Cruikshank* (Bellew Publishing, 1992), p. 143.
4. Kenneth Bird ('Fougasse'), *The Good-Tempered Pencil* (Max Reinhardt, 1956).
5. Sir Francis Carruthers Gould, quoted in Ann Gould, 'The Picture Politics of Francis Curruthers Gould', *20th Century Studies* (December 1975), p. 26.
6. Ambrose Bierce 'As to Cartooning' (1900) in *The Collected Works of Ambrose Bierce* (Gordian Press, 1966), p. 86.
7. Sir David Low, *Ye Madde Designer* (Studio, 1935), pp. 11-12.
8. Sir Ernst Gombrich, Introduction to exhibition catalogue 'The Art of Laughter' (Cartoon Art Trust, 1992), p. 11.
9. J.B.Priestley, *English Humour* (Longman, 1930), p. 49.
10. John Berger, quoted in Gerald Scarfe, *Scarfe by Scarfe* (Hamish Hamilton, 1986), p. 37.
11. Fritz Behrendt, 'The Freedom of the Political Cartoonist' in *20th Century Studies* (December 1975), p. 78.
12. Bill Tidy, *Is There Any News of the Iceberg?* (Smith Gryphon, 1995), p. 75.
13. Rt Hon. Kenneth Baker CH MP, *The Prime Ministers* (Thames & Hudson, 1995), p. 17.
14. Colin Seymour-Ure, *The Political Impact of Mass Media* (Constable, 1974), p. 257.
15. John Jensen, 'Curious! I Seem to Hear a Child Weeping!': Will Dyson (1880-1938)' in *20th Century Studies* (December 1975), p. 39.
16. Victor Weisz ('Vicky'), *The Editor Regrets* (Allan Wingate, 1947).
17. V.S.Pritchett, 'The Manhandling Democratic Touch' in Mark Bryant (ed.) *The Complete Colonel Blimp* (Bellew Publishing, 1991), pp. 156-7.

An illustration by Edmund J. Sullivan (1869-1933) from his book *The Kaiser's Garland*, which James Thorpe described as 'a wholehearted hymn of hate' (*Edmund J. Sullivan*, 1948). The writing on the wall is the familiar 'Mene, Mene, Tekel Upharsin' from the Book of Daniel, indicating here that the Kaiser's time is up.

[36] Edmund J. Sullivan, *The Kaiser's Garland*, London, 1915.

The German New Heathen

An anti-Nazi drawing by the Czech cartoonist Bert reproduced in the book *Juden Christen Heiden im III Reich* (Prague, 1935), published in German, French and English. The cartoon is subtitled 'Our Aryan myth is; "Love your neighbour – by tearing him to pieces".'

[37] Bert, *Juden Christen Heiden im III Reich*, Prague, 1935.

An anti-Semitic carton by Fips from a 1940 edition of *Der Stürmer*, the weekly Nazi newspaper edited by Julius Streicher which ran the strapline 'The Jews are our misfortune!' (*Die Juden sind unser Unglück!*) across the bottom of the front page of each issue. In this drawing 'the Jewish conspiracy' lies behind the British bomb-aimer's every action and 'Murder' is written across the sky.

[38] Fips, *Der Stürmer*, No.30, 1943.

'Thus speaketh the Lord of Hosts, saying, execute true judgment, and shew mercy...' – Zechariah, 7:9

A particularly poignant example of the work of Vicky (Victor Weisz, 1913-66). Adolf Eichmann had been one of the Nazi leaders responsible for carrying out Hitler's 'final solution' policy – the mass extermination of Jews in Europe. This cartoon was published in the *Evening Standard* on 26 May 1960, shortly after Eichmann had been discovered living in Argentina and arrested for war crimes.

[39] Vicky (Victor Weisz), *Evening Standard*, 26 May 1960.

The Price of Sovereignty has Increased – Official

In this cartoon published in the *Guardian* during the Falklands War after the sinking, in quick succession, of the Argentinian cruiser *General Belgrano* and the British ship H.M.S. *Sheffield* with great loss of life, Les Gibbard (b. 1945) harked back to the famous wartime drawing by Philip Zec (1909-83) 'The Price of Petrol Has Been Increased by One Penny – Official' which nearly led to the *Daily Mirror*'s closure. For this drawing Gibbard himself was branded a traitor by the pro-war *Sun*.

[40] Les Gibbard, *Guardian*, 6 May 1982.

A powerful cartoon by Chris Riddell (b. 1962) published in the *Independent on Sunday* to illustrate a leader about the rise of nationalism in the Balkans and Eastern Europe in the 1990s.

[41] Chris Riddell, *Independent on Sunday*.

Stiletto in the Ink: British Political Cartoons in the 1990s[1]

John Harvey

There is no more reason why one cartoonist should have much in common with another than there is why one doctor should be significantly like another doctor, but political cartoonists share certain qualities. They frequently draw with a considerable degree of passion. They appear united, whatever the differences in other political views they hold, in their dislike of pomposity and political hypocrisy. They have the capacity to produce, day after day, week after week, year after year, ideas and images and humour and to boil these down into simple and penetrating insights. They can be as ruthless as they are funny. All these are positive, in some cases almost macho, qualities.

But many cartoonists also share a remarkable degree of self-doubt about the effectiveness of their work, and the role they have on their newspapers. It is not, curiously enough, a doubt generally shared by their editors, and it is not a doubt either, the editors say, which is reflected in the size of the pay packet which cartoonists can expect to take home or spend while on their way home. Some play down their own talent, or dismiss the talents of other political cartoonists, but mostly their self-doubt about the importance of the contribution they are making is a by-product of the vast complexity and competitive world which is the media today compared with just two or three decades ago.

As JAK (Raymond Jackson), cartoonist of the *Evening Standard*, says, visual images are now instantaneous in the case of many important news events, and near enough to it in most of them. The Gulf War was channelled into viewers in mind-numbing detail. And if you want a visual image of Sarajevo, it is more or less immediately available – and in colour on the front page of your newspaper the next morning – if you missed it on television last night. When there are mortar attacks on Heathrow, or one corpse after another is uncovered in a Gloucester village, newspapers now not only shoot the scene in colour, but provide, for those who need the additional information, back-up in the form of graphic illustrations. But as JAK points out, when Low was drawing at the *Evening Standard* pictures from overseas could take days to arrive, so that frequently cartoonists provided the first visual image of an important event.

The political cartoon is only part of JAK's work, however. Heath, who draws both big political cartoons and pocket cartoons far more regularly, is more depressed about the effectiveness of his work:

> The *Evening Standard* in 1940 had four pages. Seeing Low, after NOT watching television all night, NOT surrounded by a million supplements, NOT surrounded by a million photographs, but by type, the image obviously remained much more memorable. Worse than the competition, however, is the cynicism and indifference of society. People are not concerned with discovering quality. Very few people actually care about drawing,

he says with some lugubriousness.

Cummings, who drew cartoons for the *Daily Express* and *Sunday Express* for well over forty years from 1948 and who was one of the great stable of cartoonists who worked under Beaverbrook, says it is always very difficult to tell accurately what effect cartoonists have, but he points to the enormous popularity of cartoons in readership surveys conducted by the *Express* at a time when the paper had Carl Giles and Osbert Lancaster drawing as well as himself. 'I think if the cartoonist regularly draws some political figure as a wet, the steady drip will have an effect.' In the early 1970s he was more positive still, writing in *The Cartoon History of Britain* that the cartoonist knows 'he disposes of an element of power. He can, by constant repetition, create an image of a politician to a large section of the voting public.'[2] Cummings believes that the TV programme *Spitting Image*, with its repellent images, may have had the effect of demeaning or lowering politicians in the public estimation, although the caricatures, which sometimes were well done and very amusing, were not reinforced by a script with wit.

Another who shares the common conviction about television images is Peter Brookes, a relative newcomer to the big political cartoon, though with vast experience as an illustrator for *The Times*. He suggests that people look at newspapers in a somewhat different way than they did when Low and Vicky were drawing. He is optimistic, however, that political cartoons – a point of view – still add up to something. That is a view Griffin, until recently at the *Daily Mirror* (and now with the *Daily Express*) endorses vigorously. 'I know I have been affected by cartoons in the past.' He believes that people who see a cartoon which makes a political statement will either agree or disagree with it, and he likes to feel sometimes he can have an influence on floating voters. Long-time *Observer* cartoonist Trog (Wally Fawkes) agrees, arguing that if a cartoon works, it can speed up the 'whole process of getting over an attitude'. MAC (Stan McMurtry) at the *Daily Mail* does not believe any political cartoons he draws will change anyone's political stance, but he sees all visual images, including cartoons, having the potential to influence people in a subliminal way.

Steve Bell of the *Guardian* is robust in defence of the importance of the political cartoon. 'There is more imagery around. It's interesting ... paradoxically, I disagree with saying the cartoon is now less important. I think it is in a sense more important.' He argues that while images are pouring out at people from all directions, much of what they see is 'pure, utter crap'. People have yet to come to terms with a new world of mega-visual images coming at them, and there is a real need for good pictorial news, information and comment to emerge from the dross that is concealing it.

So what do politicians think themselves about the effectiveness of cartoons on their occupation, and on the people who vote for them?

Former Conservative Prime Minister Sir Edward Heath, who like Harold Macmillan before him and John Major more recently was subjected to considerable criticism in the Tory press, is an avid collector of cartoon originals. He is doubtful whether today's cartoonists have the artistic skills of those who were drawing when he entered politics, and he doubts their impact as well. His chief concern is that cartoonists have become too narrow in their approach, too absorbed with single issues, such as John Major's leadership; though, of course, many cartoons in 1963 were thoroughly absorbed with Harold Macmillan's leadership at a time when Sir Edward himself was assuming greater prominence in the Tory Party. The most considerable doubt Sir Edward has, however, relates in a different way to television. He maintains that while cartoonists and television satirical programmes might maintain their assault on Mr Major endlessly, viewers now have so much opportunity to see politicians live on television, or being interviewed on television, that they can make up their own minds after seeing politicians as themselves rather than as caricatures.

Former Labour deputy leader Roy Hattersley, now a journalist and novelist, is another cartoon-lover who is also dubious about the influence of modern political cartooning. He thinks there is reason to believe Mr Major is upset about the underpants theme in Bell's cartoons, but he maintains that when politicians do become upset, they are treating cartoons more seriously than they should. 'Readers of a newspaper regard the cartoon as something else. It isn't part of the general comment on and criticism of politics.' The cartoon can be brilliant, and make some instant impact because of that, but in the end it remains 'a bit of a joke'. *Spitting Image*, however, has done considerable damage to Mr Major and to politicians like David Steel, and he might not have liked the programme quite so much himself 'if I had been Kenneth Baker, depicted as a slug sliming my way through life'.

The importance of the newspaper cartoon was endorsed strongly by editors Max Hastings and Peter Preston.[3] Hastings was adamant that the big cartoon can make an important statement in any newspaper, quality or tabloid, and considered the *Telegraph*'s retrieval of Garland from the *Independent* in 1991 an important success:

> We've sometimes been very critical of this government in our leader columns and in articles we write, but I honestly don't think that anything critical of Mr Major that we have said has had anything like the devastating impact of the line that Nick Garland draws, very often, in his cartoons of this weak, frightened little rabbit of a man who's Prime Minister. I think Nick Garland arguably makes a ruthless point more effectively than we would choose to do or even probably be able to do in words.

Preston was equally positive about the importance of Bell. Bell's underpants image, he said, is 'exactly the same, if you look back 30 years, as Vicky's Supermac or in a sense David Low's (TUC) carthorse. They're all images which have resonance, and fall into the language.' When Preston attended a conference in South Africa, he was struck at seeing a South African impressionist performing in cabaret and doing Major in underpants:

> This was very bizarre because 6000 miles away there was Steve's image carried on through. It's like all walks of life. A good, pungent newspaper column is better than a damp, soft, tired newspaper column. But when you've got a cartoonist operating in a rich vein, then you have the added benefit that there are all those images which register on the visual subconscious.

The *Oldie* editor Richard Ingrams, who has worked with many of today's cartoonists on *Private Eye*, believes there were more important cartoonists in the 1960s than there are today, but says a 'really good' cartoon can still alter the public's view more effectively than anything else. Simon Jenkins, former editor of both the *Evening Standard* and *The Times*, says he has always believed 'humour names its price'. On all newspapers on which he has worked, he says, the cartoonist has been an immensely important element in the paper's personality. 'People will say they buy a paper because of Garland or Vicky or JAK or whoever it might be. While that may be an exaggeration, I don't think that anyone, apart from maybe the humorous columnist, is quite as important to defining a paper's position in the world, its politics, its general personality.' Jenkins also believes that today's cartoons can still create a public image in the way Low created the carthorse image for the TUC. 'John Major's portrayal by contemporary cartoonists is something he will never really lose. It's become John Major. I think they are still very important.'

Cartoonists today still enjoy a remarkable degree of journalistic autonomy. Those who seem to have the most free hand generally work for upmarket or quality newspapers. Nick Garland says he can do whatever he likes. 'I don't think I've ever been told, "Steer clear of this subject", or "This is the line you must take on that subject". To some extent one exercises a certain self-censorship … If I have ever disobeyed my own injunctions of that sort, and done the cartoon anyway, the editor has always accepted it.' Garland says he operated under the same conditions when he worked at the *Independent*, and Michael Heath says the same applies to him now. When the paper approached him to do a big cartoon, 'the editor had to agree, if he wanted me, there was no point in criticising or being a pain in the neck, therefore giving me an entirely free rein, with the only proviso that I don't get into trouble legally'. Heath says he applies the same rules to cartoonists he uses himself at the *Spectator* as that periodical's cartoon editor, and he warns most sternly about the folly of allowing editors and other journalists to have a say in creating the idea for a cartoon. Steve Bell, in Peter Preston's words, works pretty constantly 'at the fringes of what is acceptable', and has not been without rejection, though that was some years ago, and he laughs about it now. 'There's never been any suggestions or control, they just let me get on with it, which I think is one of the great strengths about the way the *Guardian* operates.' The paper is sometimes concerned about libel – 'it's not usually politicians who are bothered, but someone on the fringes of public life who is likely to sue' – but he tends to send his cartoon in close to deadline, so there is not much time to change anything anyway.

Cartoonists on the tabloid papers work in a different way, though all are responsible for their own ideas. Cummings says nothing has changed about the way he works professionally from the time he started his career. 'We had incredible freedom under Beaverbrook. He was an exceptionally brilliant journalist. He knew people would only do their best work if they were allowed to do what they bloody well liked.' Cummings generally thinks up five or six ideas, roughs them out quickly, and shows them to his editor who chooses the one he/she likes best. 'Sometimes I think one is my best and the editor doesn't, but my wife sees them all and usually says the editor has chosen the best one.' In his early days Beaverbrook had occasionally ribbed him if he had done things Beaverbrook disagreed with, but it was a Tory paper and 'I was able to go for the Tory Party to my heart's content if I wanted to.' On the *Evening Standard* JAK produces some six roughs a day which he takes into the editor, and says libel and taste are the main areas in which he is likely to run into problems. 'The *Standard* is a very moral paper, and I can't do some of the things I see other cartoonists doing.'

For cartoonists the greatest change in newspapers in the last thirty years, apart from the vast array of visual images in modern papers and their sheer size, is the fact that upmarket newspapers now publish political cartoons on a regular basis. In 1963 Papas worked for both the *Guardian* and the *Sunday Times*, but otherwise cartoonists found their preserve in mid-market or downmarket newspapers. In fact, now the most serious political cartoonists find their outlet in the quality newspapers. The popular newspapers have some of the best cartoonists, but their drawings are often not political. The technology has also changed the work practices of some cartoonists, giving them more freedom in the way they operate. Giles used to work from his home in Suffolk and send his cartoons to the office by train. Bell did the same with his strip cartoons when he started at the *Guardian*, but the fax and computer have now extended his deadline for the big cartoon.

A comparison of today's cartoons with those of 1963 shows little difference in the subjects covered by the cartoonists, apart from the fact that many cartoons in popular papers are now not political. Perhaps the drawings of Vicky, Papas, Cummings and Illingworth on subjects such as the Cold War, Britain's entry into the EEC, nuclear test-ban treaties and civil rights in the United States might now seem to be weighty because of their historical significance compared to some of today's drawings. But today's cartoonists are dealing with the international complexities of today's world, and issues such as the changes in Russia and South Africa, the events in Sarajevo and Northern Ireland, are arguably just as important as anything that happened 30 years ago. There is really little difference between Vicky drawing a cartoon of a summit meeting in the 1960s and Brookes drawing a cartoon in 1994 showing white South African parliamentarians dreaming of a white Christmas like they used to know. The reality is that cartoonists today are just as concerned as their counterparts were in 1963 to lampoon and mock political hypocrisy, frailty, deceit, weakness and pomposity, and to become angered about social unfairness and inequality. The reality too is that some will draw cartoons today which delight with their inconsequentiality just as much as cartoonists did 30 years ago. British political cartooning remains robust.

References

1. This paper with interviews was prepared while the author was a Fellow on the Reuter Foundation programme at Green College, Oxford, in 1994. A fuller version is published in *Quiplash*, Vol III, Nos I & IV (Wellington N.Z., 1994)
2. Michael Cummings, 'How a Political Cartoonist Views his Profession', foreword to Michael Wynn Jones, *The Cartoon History of Britain* (London, Tom Stacey, 1971), p. 13.
3. Since this article was written, Max Hastings moved to the *Evening Standard* and Peter Preston became Editor-in-Chief of the *Guardian* group.

Michael Cummings: 'I think if the cartoonist regularly draws some political figure as a wet, the steady drip will have an effect.'

[42] Michael Cummings, *Daily Express*, 23 November 1980.

MAC (Stan McMurtry) does not believe any political cartoons he draws will change anyone's political stance, but he sees all visual images, including cartoons, having the potential to influence people in a subliminal way.

[43] MAC (Stan McMurtry), *Daily Mail*, 17 May 1974.

Peter Preston:
David Low's carthorse is an image 'which has resonance, and falls into the language'.

[44] David Low, *Evening Standard*, 21 August 1947.

Trog (Wally Fawkes):
If a cartoon works, it can speed up the 'whole process of getting over an attitude'.

[45] Trog (Wally Fawkes), *London Daily News*, 19 May 1987.

Perhaps the drawings of Vicky, Papas, Cummings and Illingworth on subjects such as the Cold War, Britain's entry into the EEC, nuclear test-ban treaties and civil rights in the United States might now seem to be weighty because of their historical significance, as compared to some of today's drawings.

[46] Leslie Illingworth; 'Childe Roland to the dark power came', *Punch*, 23 February 1955.

Preston: Bell's underpants image is 'exactly the same, if you look back 30 years, as Vicky's Supermac.'

[47] Vicky (Victor Weisz), *Evening Standard*, 6 November 1958.

[48] Steve Bell, *IF . . .Kicks Butt* (Methuen, London, 1990-1), p. 133.

Contributors

Steve Bell started his cartooning career for *Whoopee!* comics, moving on to the *New Statesman*, *Time Out* and *City Limits*, among many other publications. His series 'Maggie's Farm' appeared in *Time Out* in 1979. Since 1981 he has drawn the political strip 'IF...' and, more recently, the editorial cartoons for the *Guardian*. Some 1000 of his early cartoons are held at the Centre.

Mark Bryant has edited many cartoon books, including acclaimed biographies of David Low, Vicky and Ronald Searle. He is the author of *World War II in Cartoons* and the *Dictionary of British Cartoonists and Caricaturists 1730-1980* (with Simon Heneage), and is Honorary Secretary of the British Cartoonists' Association.

Nicholas Garland drew the strip 'Barry Mackenzie', written by Barry Humphries and published in *Private Eye* 1964-74. In 1966 he became the first political cartoonist for the *Daily Telegraph* where he has remained, apart from a brief period for the *Independent* from 1986-91. He has also drawn regularly for the *New Statesman*, the *Spectator* and *Investors Chronicle*. An admirer of Vicky, he has been voted Cartoonist of the Year twice by Granada TV (1972, 1987). The Centre holds some 5000 of his cartoons.

John Harvey is editor of the *Evening Standard* in Palmerston North, New Zealand. In 1994 he was awarded a grant by the David Low Fellowship to spend a term on the Reuter Foundation Programme at Green College, Oxford. During his time in the UK, he took the opportunity to interview many British cartoonists.

John Jensen has been a professional cartoonist since 1947. He arrived in England from Australia in 1950 and his cartoons have appeared in a wide variety of publications – most notably *Punch*, *Spectator*, *Tatler* and the *Sunday Telegraph*. His cartoons have ranged from social to sport, from theatre to political. He has been Chairman of the Cartoon Art Trust and is currently Chairman of the British Cartoonists' Association. The Centre holds over 1500 of his cartoons.

Kevin Kallaugher (KAL) graduated from Harvard in 1977 and came to England on a bicycle tour. In 1978 he became the *Economist*'s first resident caricaturist and since then his cartoons have appeared in many UK newspapers. Syndicated worldwide, he has been editorial cartoonist for the *Baltimore Sun* in the USA since 1988. The Centre holds some 700 of his cartoons published in British newspapers.

Roger Law is best known for his long-standing partnership with Peter Fluck, which culminated in the 'Spitting Image' animated caricature puppet programme for TV (1982-96). Caricaturist, poster/mural artist, journalist, lecturer and film-maker, Law continues to work from Cairo Studios in London.

Ralph Steadman – besides being a film director, stage designer, stamp designer, and writer of libretti – has appeared as a cartoonist in a wide variety of publications since 1959. He has illustrated and written many books (his latest being George Orwell's *Animal Farm*), has exhibited worldwide and has received many awards. In 1995 he was honoured by the University of Kent with a DLitt. The Centre holds some 200 of his early cartoons.

Editorial Board: Robert Edwards, Jane Newton, Colin Seymour-Ure, David Welch

This book was sponsored by a University of Kent Development Trust Grant, and produced by the University of Kent Printing Unit. Editorial correspondence should be sent to the Director, The Centre for the Study of Cartoons and Caricature, Templeman Library, University of Kent at Canterbury, Canterbury, Kent CT2 7NU, UK.

Acknowledgements

For permission to reproduce the cartoons in this anthology The Centre for the Study of Cartoons and Caricature wishes to thank the following:

John Jensen: [1, 2, 3, 4, 5, 6, 7, 8] plus own caricature
Ralph Steadman: cover, frontispiece, [9, 10, 11, 12, 13, 14] plus own caricature
Steve Bell: [15, 16, 17, 18, 19, 20, 21, 22, 23, 48] plus own caricature
Solo Syndication and Literary Agency: [24, 39, 43, 44, 47] plus back cover illustration
Ewan MacNaughton/*Daily Telegraph*: [25]
Nicholas Garland: [26, 27] plus own caricature
Roger Law/*Spitting Image*: [28, 29, 30, 31, 32] plus own caricature
Kevin Kallaugher/*Baltimore Sun*: [33, 34, 35] plus own caricature
Les Gibbard: [40]
Chris Riddell: [41]
Express Newspapers: [42]
Wally Fawkes: [45]
Punch: [46]

Attempts have been made to trace all copyright-holders. Advice on any omissions would be appreciated and they will be corrected in future editions.

UNIVERSITY OF KENT
AT CANTERBURY ■■■■

Officially inaugurated in 1975, The Centre for the Study of Cartoons and Caricature is the only collection of its kind in Western Europe. Its archival resource is an amalgamation of more than 80,000 original cartoon drawings and comprises work deposited by the Beaverbrook Foundation, Associated Newspapers and The Mirror Group, as well as by individual cartoonists and private donors. The cartoons have been published in the British national press since 1904.

Holdings include original work by W.K. Haselden, Sidney 'George' Strube, Percy Fearon ('Poy'), E.H. Shepard, Will Dyson, David Low, Victor Weisz ('Vicky'), Michael Cummings, Leslie Illingworth, James Friell ('Gabriel'), Tom Webster, John Jensen, Nicholas Garland, Ralph Steadman and Steve Bell, among many others.

Deposited cartoons are photographed and catalogued into the Centre's computer database, a record (part of which is now on CD-ROM) which is readily accessible to researchers. This record is reinforced by a comprehensive library of books on cartoons, caricature, socio-political humour and satire, as well as historical biographies, cartoon anthologies, treatises and various research papers.

The collection and database are used extensively by an ever-widening constituency which includes local, national and international book publishers, TV and print editors and journalists, librarians, museum and gallery curators, university and school staff, teaching-aid designers, students, authors, art/heritage administrators, history and popular culture enthusiasts and cartoonists themselves.

For additional information please write to the Director, The Centre for the Study of Cartoons and Caricature, University of Kent at Canterbury, Canterbury, Kent CT2 7NU, UK.